Beasts and Beauties

EIGHT TALES FROM EURO

Carol Ann Duffy was born in Glasgow and gre.. up in Stafford. She won the 1993 Whitbread Award for Poetry and the Forward Prize for best collection for *Mean Time*. *The World's Wife* received the E. M. Forster Award in America, while *Rapture* won the T. S. Eliot Prize 2005. She is currently Professor of Contemporary Poetry at Manchester Metropolitan University. *Beasts and Beauties* is her fourth collaboration, in theatre or opera, with Tim Supple and Melly Still. Her most recent volumes of poetry are *New and Collected Poems for Children* (2009) and *The Bees* (2011), which won the Costa Poetry Award, and her edited volume, *Jubilee Lines* (2012). She is Poet Laureate.

Melly Still has worked as a director, choreographer, designer and adaptor for many companies including the National Theatre, the RSC, Glyndebourne, Bristol Old Vic, Hampstead and the Young Vic. Her work has travelled throughout the UK, Europe, the Far East and Broadway. She is collaborating with Carol Ann Duffy on a production of *The Pied Piper* for Manchester Royal Exchange. *Beasts and Beauties* is one of eighteen creative collaborations with Tim Supple.

Tim Supple has directed, adapted and devised theatre, opera and film throughout the UK and in the US, Europe, India and the Middle and Far East. He has worked regularly at the National Theatre and the Royal Shakespeare Company. In the 1990s he was Artistic Director of the Young Vic in London. His current company, Dash Arts, creates new theatre, music, dance and visual art in collaboration with artists from abroad. Between 2006 and 2008 his multi-lingual Indian *A Midsummer Night's Dream* played across four continents and his most recent production of *One Thousand and One Nights*, created in the Arab world between 2009 and 2011, premiered at the Luminato Festival of Toronto and the Edinburgh International Festival before going on tour.

BEASTS AND BEAUTIES

Eight Tales from Europe

retold by
CAROL ANN DUFFY

adapted by
MELLY STILL *and* TIM SUPPLE

faber and faber

First published in 2004
by Faber and Faber Limited
Bloomsbury House 74–77 Great Russell Street,
London WC1B 3DA

Typeset by Country Setting, Kingsdown, Kent CT14 8ES
Printed and boud by CPI Group (UK) Ltd, Croydon, CR0 4YY
All rights reserved

A CIP record for this book
is available from the British Library

ISBN 978–0–571–22669–6

8 10 9 7

For Ella, Rosie and Annie
Felix, Olive and Iris
with love

Contents

Introduction

This collection retells a handful of Europe's best-known and loved tales and throws in a few surprises. There are two texts for each story: Carol Ann Duffy's prose and our dramatisation. For the stories to strike deeply the hearts of all ages, they must be works of literature of the finest quality and for the theatre production of *Beasts and Beauties* Carol Ann's versions were our starting point. The dramatisations are essentially the stories stripped of description, leaving the bare events to resonate. The tales are faithful to the originals, our shared aim being to retell rather than to reinterpret.

We are often asked how we decided on the eight in this collection. After reading several hundred folk and fairy tales from almost every country across Europe, we eventually agreed on a shortlist, the 'finalists' of which shared a particular quality. Most of these ancient tales when read ignite the imagination. We might be enthralled by descriptions of weird creatures and terrible fears or captivated by rhythms and repetitions on the page. But for a story to unfurl its magic on stage the crucial ingredients are those of drama: character choice and development, tension, conflict, narrative economy and a satisfying dramatic structure. Sumptuous settings, atmospheric music and vigorous action can't compensate for lack of drama. This collection is brimming with dramatic possibility. And variety. Each tale can be defined by its genre: the thriller *Blue Beard*, the farce *The Husband Who Was to Mind the House*, the fairy tale *Three Wishes*, the romance *Beauty and the Beast*, the satire *The Emperor's New Clothes*, the folk tale *Toby and the Wolf* and a tale of magic *The North Wind*. *The Juniper Tree* shifts from the lyrical to the Brechtian to the operatic with a good deal of horror.

The stories originate from different countries but this is all we can say for certain about their beginnings as they probably evolved orally. And in our imaginations each insistently rooted itself in a particular period of history. So *Blue Beard* becomes a tale sensationalised in the salons of Napoleonic France; the Italian *Beauty and the Beast* becomes a Renaissance romance; *Toby and the Wolf*, originally a Bohemian folk tale, finds itself transported to Soviet Czechoslovakia; *The Emperor's New Clothes* poses as a story about a contemporary European monarchy encroached upon by two anachronistic weavers. These thoughts we shared with Carol Ann, who promptly infused the stories with her impressions, and the countries' personalities now dance off the page.

Although we delight in the character of a country, one of the great appeals of this collection is the simple voice, indifferent to nations and borders, that seeks to communicate the human experience: joy and despair, birth and death, failure and success, love and loss. And more complex social issues communicated in ways easily assimilated by young children, such as parental cruelty, sibling rivalry, jealousy, poverty, marriage, sex and murder. We've always intended that the production should appeal to people of all ages, assuming that any member of the audience regardless of age is as sophisticated as the next.

The title of the production and therefore this collection is two-toned. *Eight Tales from Europe* may light the fire of my forty-(odd)-year-old-imagination by evoking the BBC2 black-and-white series of a similar name (*Tales from Europe*), but Bristol's discerning artistic directors, too young to have been transported by *The Singing Ringing Tree,* argued that any mention of Europe in 2004 brings to mind the EU! So *Beasts and Beauties* was born to the delight of all involved.

In dramatising the stories our aim was to maintain their core form and remain faithful to the original narrative voice. Above all, the intimate relationship between teller and listener needed to stay intact in order simply, directly and powerfully to communicate these remarkable tales. Eight actors (four men and four women) share the stories and the narrative voice which shifts from story to story and often within a story. The narrator is often the protagonist, speaking of him or herself in the third person and past tense while being thrust inexorably by the force of words into the here and now, e.g. the husband (*The Husband Who Was to Mind the House*), the woodman (*The Three Wishes*), the bride (*Blue Beard*) and Kari (*The North Wind*). At other times the narrator is a character on the edge of the central story: a neighbour (*Blue Beard*), the nursemaid (*Toby and the Wolf*), the stonemason (*The Juniper Tree),* bound to watch and recall again and again the hero's or heroine's misery, unable to change the course of events, compelling them to endure, fall and finally conquer. Or the narrator may be more conventionally detached from the story in the once-upon-a-time mould, as in *Beauty and the Beast*, though less conventionally she is supported by two characters (we call them Fates 1 and 2) whose words and actions steer the fate of the protagonists. At other times throughout, the narration functions as dialogue.

The set, costumes, props, lighting, music and action paint for us a sense of history, place, social status, thought and feeling. This is why the dramatisation delivers the stories as if they've shed several layers of clothing. They get dressed again once they're on stage. The omitted text is restored by the actions of characters in the flesh, by living objects, by music, colour, light. But during rehearsals we were never without the complete stories. They inform, give detail and provide stage directions for everyone involved.

The performance of *Beasts and Beauties: Eight Tales from Europe* lasts about one hour and forty five minutes with an interval. The running order was very carefully considered. There were four stories in each half. The changes between each story were swift, often playful and always musical.

Melly Still, 2004

Beasts and Beauties was produced and performed at Bristol Old Vic Theatre in April 2004 and then at Hampstead Theatre in December 2010 and 2011.

The show was first produced as *Dumme Konge og Grimme Troll* at Norway's Den Nationale Scene in Bergen. The stories (predating Carol Ann Duffy's versions) were translated by Tale Næss.

Beasts and Beauties

EIGHT TALES FROM EUROPE

Dramatised by
Tim Supple and Melly Still

Blue Beard

Narrator/Neighbour 1 Once upon a time, there lived a man who owned many splendid properties in the town and in the country, who possessed an abundance of silver and gold plate, hand-crafted furniture, the finest porcelain and glass . . .

Narrator/Neighbour 2 But he was the owner of something else as well – a blue beard which made him so appallingly ugly that women and girls took one look at him and fled.

Mother He had a neighbour, a society lady, who had two fine sons and two daughters who were flowers of beauty. He asked her for one of the girls' hand in marriage.

Daughter 1 Neither of the girls would have him, though, and they sent him backwards

Daughter 2 and forwards,

Daughter 1 up,

Daughter 2 down, and sideways

Daughter 1 from one

Daughter 2 to the other,

Daughter 1 both adamant they would not marry a man with a blue beard.

Daughter 2 But there was something else which repelled them even more. He had already been married to several wives and no one living knew what had happened to them.

Narrator / Neighbour 1 The Blue Beard, to try and win them over, escorted them with their mama and brothers, and other fine young people of the district, to one of his country estates,

Narrator / Neighbour 2 where they were entertained for eight sumptuous days.

Narrator / Neighbour 1 So now it was all music and masks.

Mother It was hunting and shooting and fishing.

Brother 1 It was the finest champagne and armagnac.

All *Santé!*

Brother 2 And dancing!

They dance.

Daughter 1 *Merci, monsieur.*

Blue Beard *Enchanté.*

All Women Ooh la la!

Daughter 1 In fact, everything went so splendidly that the youngest daughter started to think that the lord of the manor's beard wasn't actually *bleu, mais non*, not really, and that he was a most civilised gentleman.

Narrator / Neighbour 1 No sooner were they home than the marriage was held.

Blue Beard A month after that, the Blue Beard told his wife that he had to travel to a distant country for at least six weeks, on a matter of extreme importance. He encouraged her to amuse herself while he was away. She was to send for her family, friends and acquaintances, and generally have a good time.

Here are the keys to the two Great Rooms that contain my best and most costly furniture; these grant access to my silver and gold plate, which is to be used sparingly; these open my strong chests, which hold all my money; these my casket of jewels; and this here is the master key that opens all my apartments. But this little one here is the key to the closet at the far end of the great gallery. Open everything and go anywhere, but do not unlock the little closet. I forbid you this – and I want you to know that I forbid you so solemnly that if you disobey me, you can seek no refuge from my outrage.

Bride (Daughter 1) She promised to do everything just as he said and so he held her to him. (*He exits.*)

Narrator/Neighbour 1 Her friends and family didn't wait to be invited –

Narrator/Neighbour 2 They were so impatient to see all the splendour of the newlyweds' house.

Narrator/Neighbour 1 Only her brothers didn't come because their military duties delayed them.

Mother But all the others rushed straight to the two great rooms,

Sister (Daughter 2) flinging wide all the closets and wardrobes to gape and coo at the finery.

Narrator/Neighbour 2 They could not say enough about their friend's good fortune.

Bride She, however, paid not the slightest attention to all the treasures, because she was burning up with curiosity about the little closet.

Narrator/Neighbour 1 She became so consumed by this, that without even thinking how rude it was to abandon her guests, she rushed down the back stairs so recklessly that she could have broken her slender neck three times over.

Bride When she reached the closet door, she paused for quite a while,

Narrator/Neighbour 1 remembering her husband's words.

Bride But temptation was far too strong for her. She picked out the little key and opened the door. At first, she could make out nothing clearly at all, because the shutters were all closed. But after a few moments she saw that the floor was spattered with lumps of congealed blood, and upon it were the bodies of dead women, each sprawled or hanging there in her wedding gown. These were the brides that the Blue Beard had married and had slaughtered one after another. (*She screams.*)

Narrator/Neighbour 1 The key fell from her hand. She tried to calm herself. Picked up the key. Locked the door.

Bride Hurried up the stairs to her chamber to try to recover.

Narrator/Neighbour 1 But she was too frightened.

Bride Then she noticed that the key to the closet was stained with blood.

Narrator/Neighbour 1 She tried three times to scrub it off.

Bride But the blood would not come off even though she scoured it with soap and sand. When she rubbed the blood from one side it would appear again on the other.

Narrator/Neighbour 2 That evening, when her guests said their *au revoirs* she begged her sister to stay.

Sister Unexpectedly Blue Beard came home. He'd interrupted his journey.

Bride His wife did everything to act as though she was delighted by his sudden return.

Blue Beard He asked her for the keys. (*She gives him the keys.*) Why is it that the key to the closet is missing?

Bride Oh! I must have left it upstairs on the table. After going backwards and forwards several times,

Blue Beard she was forced to bring him the key. How did this blood get on the key?

Bride I don't know.

Blue Beard You don't know, you don't know; but I know. You were determined to go into the closet, weren't you? Very well, madame, you shall go in, and take your place among the sisterhood you found there.

Bride Forgive me, I swear, I'm sorry. I'll never disobey you again.

Narrator/Neighbour 1 Even a stone would have been moved by her beauty and grief.

Narrator/Neighbour 2 But the Blue Beard's heart was harder than any stone.

Blue Beard You must die, *chérie*, and soon.

Bride If I have to die, then allow me a little time to dress in my bridal shroud.

Blue Beard You may have a quarter of an hour, but not a second longer.

Bride As soon as she was alone, she called to her sister. Sister, climb to the top of the tower and see if my brothers are coming. They promised to come today. If you see them, give them a sign to hurry.

Sister Her sister went to the top of the tower.

Bride Do you see anything?

Sister I see nothing but the sun making dust.

Blue Beard Sharper, sharper, shiny knife, cut the throat of whiny wife! Come down at once or I'll come up to you!

Bride Just one moment longer, please. First I have to fasten my corselage and put on my silken stockings. Sister, Sister, do you see anything coming?

Sister I see nothing but the sun making dust and the grass growing green.

Blue Beard Sharply, sharply, knife so dear, slit her throat from ear to ear! Get down here now, or I'll come up to you.

Bride I'm coming. I just have to tie my garter and slip on my shoes. Sister, Sister, do you see anything coming?

Sister I see . . . a great dust rolling in.

Bride Is it my brothers?

Sister Oh, no, my dear sister! It's just a flock of sheep.

Blue Beard Now the knife is sharp enough, and ready for the bloody stuff! Get down here now! Or I'll come up to you!

Bride One last moment. I have only my veil to secure and my white kid gloves. Sister, do you see anything coming?

Sister I can see two horsemen coming, but they are still a long way off.

Bride Thanks be to God.

Sister It is our brothers! I have made them a sign to make great haste.

Blue Beard The Blue Beard roared out now so loudly that the whole house shook.

She collapses at his feet, sobbing.

This won't help. You must die.

He grasps her hair with one hand and raises the cutlass with the other. He is about to cut off her head . . .

Bride Please! One last moment to collect myself.

Blue Beard No, no, no. Give yourself over to God!

Narrator/Neighbour 1 At this exact moment there came such a thunderous knocking at the gates that the Blue Beard froze.

Narrator/Neighbour 2 The two horsemen entered.

Brother 1 They saw the Blue Beard,

Brother 2 and drew their swords.

Narrator/Neighbour 2 Blue Beard ran for his life.

Fight. Blue Beard is killed.

Brother 2 And they left him there dead.

Narrator/Neighbour 1 Their poor sister was scarcely more alive than her husband and was too weak to stand and embrace her brothers.

Narrator/Neighbour 2 The Blue Beard had no heirs and so his wife became owner of all his estate.

Sister With one part, she gave a dowry to her sister, to marry a young gentleman who had loved her truly for a long time.

Brother 1 Another part she used to buy captains' commissions for her brothers.

Bride And she used the rest to marry herself to a very kind gentleman, who soon made her forget the dark time she had spent with the Blue Beard.

The Husband
Who Was to Mind the House

Blue Beard (*having removed beard*) Now you're going to meet a husband from Norway.

Goody A man once stomped about northern parts who was so grumpy and surly that he thought his wife could do nothing right in the house.

Husband So one evening, during harvest time, he came cursing, blowing and fuming home, showing his teeth and kicking up a right dust.

Goody My love, you mustn't be so angry. Tomorrow why don't we swap our work? I'll go out with the mowers and mow, and you can keep house at home.

Husband Yes, that would do nicely.

Goody So, first thing next morning, his goody put the scythe over her neck and walked out into the hayfield with the mowers and set off mowing.

Husband And the man was to stay at home, mind the house, and do the housework. His first task was to churn the butter, but when he had churned for a bit, he worked up a thirst, and went to the cellar to tap a barrel of ale.

Pig enters.

But just as he was fitting the tap to the cask, he heard the pig lumber into the kitchen. So he legged it as fast as he could, to sort out the pig before it knocked over the churn. And there it stood, snuffling and rooting in the cream, which was pouring all over the floor.

The Husband becomes so mad with rage that he
forgets about the ale-barrel and charges at the Pig as
hard as he can. He catches it and fetches it such kicks
that the Pig lies for dead.

Then he remembered he had the tap in his hand; but
when he ran to the cellar, every last drop of ale had
dripped out of the cask.

Cow enters.

So he found enough left-over cream to fill the churn
again, for there'd better be butter at dinner.

Cow Moooooo.

Husband He remembered their milking cow.

Cow Moooooo.

He milks her.

Cow Moooooo.

Husband She hadn't been fed or watered all morning.
But it was too far to the meadow, so he'd just put her up
on the top of the house. The house, you should realise,
had a roof which was thatched with sods and a good
crop of grass had sprouted up there. The house was built
close to a steep slope and he reckoned that if he laid a
plank across to the thatch at the back, he'd get the cow
up, no problem.

He attempts to lead her up. Meanwhile Baby enters.

Baby Waaa.

Husband But he still couldn't leave the churn because
there was his baby crawling around on the floor.

Baby Dadda?

Husband The child is sure to knock it over. (*He heaves the churn onto his back.*)

Cow Mooo.

Husband Then he thought he'd best water the cow before he put her up on the thatch; so he picked up a bucket to draw water from the well.

As he bends over the mouth of the well, all the cream pours out of the churn and vanishes into the well.

Cow Mooo.

Eventually the Cow is coerced onto the roof.

Husband It was getting near dinner-time, so he decided he'd better boil up the porridge, so he put the porridge pot over the fire.

Cow Mooo.

Husband But he worried that the cow might fall off the roof and break her neck, so he tied one end of the rope round the cow's neck, and the other end he slid down the chimney and tied it round his own ankle. And he had to get a move on, because the oats were bubbling away.

He starts to stir, but the Cow falls off the top of the house, and drags the man up the chimney by the leg. He is stuck there like a cork in a bottle while the Cow dangles between heaven and earth, unable to get either up or down.

Goody Meanwhile, the goody had been waiting seven lengths and seven widths of the field for her husband to call them to dinner, but no call came. Finally, she reckoned she'd worked and waited long enough. The moment she got home she saw the ugly sight of the swinging cow, so she cut the rope in two. As soon as she did this, her husband came falling down out of the chimney.

Cacophony of Husband, Cow, Pig and Baby.

When his old dame came into the kitchen, there she found her baby cradling the half-dead pig and the husband standing on his brainbox in the porridge pot.

She pulls his head up, covered in porridge.

This is what happened the day the husband was to mind the house.

The Three Wishes

Wood-Wife Have any of you ever had a wish come true? Well, let us tell you about a poor woodman who dwelled in a great English forest a very long time ago, and who one day met a real fairy.

Woodman Every day that the woodman lived, out he went to fell timber.

Wood-Wife One fine day, the wood-wife packed his pouch and looped his bottle over his shoulder, and off he went, into the forest.

Woodman He had his eye on a huge old oak, reckoning it would yield strong planks aplenty. When he stood beneath it, out came his axe and around his bonce it swung.

Fairy Please please please!

The Woodman, unable to see the fairy, hesitates, then prepares to swing again.

Please! Spare the tree!

When he sees the fairy, he is stunned and speechless. At last he finds his tongue.

Woodman Well . . . I'll do as thou wants.

Fairy You have done yourself a greater favour than you know, and I propose to show my gratitude by granting you your next three wishes, whatever they may be. At that, the fairy was nowhere to be seen and the woodman loped for home.

Woodman Well, the way was a long one and the poor man was flummoxed and flabbergasted by the magical thing that had happened to him. But when he got home there was nowt in his noddle but a strong desire to plonk himself down in his chair and rest.

Fairy Perhaps this was the work of the fairy? Your guess.

Woodman Anyroad, as he sat next to the toasty fire he grew hungry: Has thou owt for supper, wife?

Wood-Wife Nowt for a couple of hours yet.

Woodman Aah! I wish I had a long strong link of black pudding in front of my face! Bonk, slither, clatter and clunk, what should fall down the chimney but a long strong link of the finest black pudding a man's heart could desire.

Wood-Wife What's happened here?

Woodman Then the woodman remembered the morning's events and he told his story from start to finish. And the woodwife glowered and glared.

Wood-Wife Thou fool! Thou fool! Thou fool! I wish the pudding was on your nose, I really do! And before you could say Flingo Macbingo, the man's neb was longer by a noble length of black pudding.

Husband He gave it a tug.

Fairy But it stuck.

Wood-Wife Then she gave it a yank.

Fairy But it stuck.

Husband *and* **Wood-Wife** And they both pulled it till it nearly tore off his nose.

Fairy But it stuck and it stuck and it stuck.

Woodman What's to happen now?

Wood-Wife (*gives him a good looking-over*) It doesn't look that bad. I wish . . .

Woodman (*interrupting*) Then the woodman realised that he must wish and wish quick; and his wish was for the black pudding to be off his conk. Alleluia! There it gleamed on the table.

Fairy And the woodman and wood-wife never rode in a fairy-tale coach or danced in satin and silk. But that evening . . .

Wood-Wife . . . they had as splendid a link of long strong black pudding as ever the heart of a man or a woman could wish for.

Beauty and the Beast

Narrator Once upon a time, there was a rich merchant who had three daughters. The girls were just as clever as they were *bella*, and none more so than the youngest, whose name was Beauty. Her sisters were jealous of her. They swanned about going to parties and pageants and jeered at Beauty because she liked to stay at home with her books. Many suitors came to court the three girls. The two eldest trilled that they would consider betrothal to nothing below a count! So there.

Beauty, in her turn, gently thanked the eligible young men but chose to remain in her father's house for a while yet.

One dark day, the merchant lost all his fortune.

Merchant We must all move at once to the country and work for our living.

Sister 2 This was a dreadful shock to the girls,

Sister 1 who had never lifted a dainty finger in their lives.

Narrator Beauty got up at first light to cook, clean, make, mend, tidy, scour and scrub.

Beauty But she made sure she read her books too.

Narrator And in less than a couple of months she was fitter and bonnier than ever. Her two sisters, however, did nothing but whine and whinge.

Sister 1 What about our fine frocks and fancy friends? And look at her!

Sister 2 How snide she is to be happy with such an awful life!

Merchant But Beauty's father was proud of his hard-working, modest daughter.

Narrator A grim year passed, then, one morning,

Merchant the merchant received news of the safe arrival of one of his ships that had been thought lost.

Sister 1 Bring us a wardrobe of expensive dresses!

Sister 2 Watch us shimmy back to society in high style!

Beauty Father's money would hardly stretch to one gown each . . . (*seeing her sisters' contempt*) Father, bring me a rose.

Merchant The merchant set off to reclaim his cargo,

Fate 1 but there were debts to be paid

Fate 2 and legal matters to settle.

Merchant He had to head for home as penniless as before.

Narrator As he returned through the Great Forest,

Fate 1 a blinding snowstorm, like a frenzy of torn-up paper money, raged

Fate 2 and he lost his way!

Merchant It is foolhardy to struggle on, but if I stay put I freeze to death. Already the wolves have sniffed me out.

Narrator Exhausted and on the lip of despair, he saw –

Merchant Thank God!

Narrator – a light in the distance,

Fates *and* **Merchant** and ran, ran for his life

Narrator until he reached a magnificent castle.

Merchant The doors were open. Hello!

A table is laid for one.

I hope the master here or his servants will forgive this intrusion!

Narrator He ate with gusto and after a glass of vino or four

Merchant he plucked up the courage to explore the castle. And came to a room with the softest, plumpest of beds in it.

Fate 2 He lay down,

Merchant tired to his bones,

Fate 2 and fell fast asleep.

Fate 1 Late next morning he was awakened by a rich scent.

Merchant Hot chocolate and sweet biscotti! This castle must belong to a kind spirit who has taken pity on me! *Grazzi*, dear good spirit!

Fate 1 Outside, instead of snow,

Merchant was the most beautiful rose garden anyone with eyes under his eyebrows had ever seen. Recalling Beauty's request,

Fate 2 he stepped outside

Merchant to pick her a rose.

Narrator The sweet, heady perfume of an opening red rose drew him towards it.

He snaps its stem. Suddenly he is nearly deafened by the roar of the Beast charging at him.

Beast Ungrateful man! I have saved your life by letting you into my castle and to thank me you steal one of my roses, which I prize over everything! You have one quarter of an hour before you meet death!

Merchant My Lord, I beg you to pardon me! Believe me, I didn't know I would offend you by picking a rose for my youngest daughter!

Beast My name is not My Lord. Don't flatter me. My name is Beast. You say you have daughters. I will spare your life on one condition – that one of them comes here of her own free will and suffers for your sake. Swear that if none of your daughters offers to die in your place you will return here within three months.

Narrator The merchant had no intention of sacrificing one of his girls, but he thought that by agreeing to the bargain he could at least say a proper goodbye to them.

Merchant He swore on oath to return.

Narrator And then he left the castle with as much despair as he had entered it with relief. By the time the moon was up, the good man was home. (*He holds out the rose.*)

Merchant Take it, Beauty. Though you cannot imagine the price I must pay for it. He told them his terrible tale.

Sister 1 So much for her pride!

Sister 2 She couldn't just ask for pretty dresses like we did.

Sister 1 Oh no!

Sister 2 Miss Goody Two-Shoes had to distinguish her stuck-up saintly self and now she would be the death of our poor father.

Sister 1 And look at her! Completely dry-eyed!

Sister 2 How callous!

Sisters How heartless!

Beauty Why should I shed any tears? If the monster will take any one of us then I will volunteer to quench his fury. Giving my father his life will prove my love for him.

Merchant Don't even think of it. I am old and my life is nearly done. I cannot accept this precious gift.

Beauty But he had to agree.

Sister 1 Her two sisters were well pleased.

Sister 2 Beauty's goodness drove them crazy and they were glad to be shot of her.

Narrator And when the day came for Beauty to leave, they had to scrub at each other's eyes with an onion to squeeze out a few tears.

Merchant The merchant and his youngest child journeyed to the castle

Beauty and discovered in the great hall, a table plentifully laid for two. The Beast wants to fatten me up before he devours me.

Beast enters.

I have come of my own free will.

Beast You are good. And I appreciate this, honest man. Get on your way now and take this chest of gold to buy costly silks for your other daughters. Don't ever think of returning here.

The Beast vanishes.

Merchant Oh, Beauty, I am scared half out of my wits for you. Let me be the one to stay!

Beauty No!

She hugs him. He cries bitterly as he leaves.

Narrator Now the poor girl was all alone for her last few hours.

Beauty She wandered through the fine castle, noticing every charming thing.

Fate 1 Before long she came to a door

Fate 2 above which was written her own name.

Beauty Inside was a wonderful collection of books that made her gasp with pleasure. Her eye fell on a book of gold.

> Welcome, Beauty.
> Have no fear.
> You are Queen and govern here.
> Say your heart's desires aloud,
> Your secret wishes.
> Don't be proud.

My only wish is to see my father.

Narrator No sooner had the words left her lips than she noticed a mirror and was amazed to see within it her father arriving home, safe but almost broken with grief. Her sisters were pretending to share his sorrow.

Beauty A moment later the image faded and was gone.

Fate 1 She drifted out into the garden

Beauty to luxuriate in the perfumes of her favourite flowers.

A hideous noise makes her jump, and she exclaims with shock as she finds herself staring straight into the eyes of Beast. Blood drips from his teeth and in his jaws is the raw flesh of a fresh-killed animal. Beauty freezes. Beast's naked shape cringes in unspeakable shame and a heart-stopping wail fills the night as he flees.

Narrator Beauty could not remember how she had got to her bedchamber that night. When she awoke in the morning she thought the whole frightful incident had been a nightmare.

Beauty There was a note. 'From now on you shall walk in the gardens undisturbed.'

Narrator The next night at supper

Beauty Beast was there, dressed in his best *capa*.

He is courteous and tries his best to display excellent table manners. But the noises he makes disgust her.

Beast Forgive me, Beauty.

Beauty nods.

If my presence distresses you, I will leave at once. Do I revolt you?

Beauty I cannot lie. You do. But I know you are very . . . good-natured.

Beast Yes. Even so, I am a monster.

Beauty There are plenty who deserve that name more than you do. I prefer you to someone who conceals a twisted heart behind an upright form.

Beast I am grateful to you. Beauty? Will you consent to be my wife?

Beauty No, Beast.

Beast screams.

Time passed.

Narrator Compassion grew like a rose and the weed of revulsion withered.

Beauty Each evening Beast came to her and they were good companions.

Narrator She had grown used to his grotesque features. Only one thing troubled her.

Beauty Every night the monster asked if she would be his wife.

Narrator One evening she said to him:

Beauty Beast, your question makes me anxious. I wish I could agree to marry you, but I can't. I shall always be fond of you as a friend. Please try to be happy with that.

Beast I ought to be happy as we are because I know how badly I'm afflicted. I value friendship, too, but I love you, Beauty. Promise me this: you will never leave me.

Beauty I promise. But if I don't see my father again, I shall never be happy.

Beast I would rather die than make you unhappy.

Beauty I swear to you that I will return in one week.

Beast Then you shall be there in the morning. When you want to come back to me, lay this ring on a table before you fall asleep. *Arrivaderci*, Beauty.

Narrator When she awoke the next day,

Beauty Beauty was in her father's house.

25

Merchant He thought he would die of shock and happiness when he saw his treasured Beauty. He summoned her two sisters, who had moved to town with their new husbands.

Fate 1 (*as Husband*) The eldest had married a gorgeous gentleman, but he fancied himself so much he never looked at her.

Fate 2 (*as Husband*) The second had wed a man famed for his wit, but he only used it now to torment and torture his wife.

Narrator Beauty's sisters nearly fell down with envy when they saw her glowing like a princess.

Sister 2 Sister, I have an idea. Let's try to keep Miss Perfect here for more than a week and, who knows, the stupid monster will be so angry she didn't keep her promise that he'll eat her.

Sister 1 Excellent! We must show her as much kindness as we can.

Narrator Their younger sister was truly touched and when the week was over she was easily won over by their tears and entreaties. So the family enjoyed more precious days together.

Beauty But as each one passed Beauty felt more and more anxious about deserting Beast. It wasn't just that she'd broken her promise. She remembered his kind heart. And the look in his eyes when she turned down his offer of marriage. It's not his fault he's so hideous. And I know I'd be much happier with him than my sisters are with their husbands. (*She remembers the ring.*)

Narrator When she awoke the next morning . . .

Beauty . . . she felt true joy at being back in Beast's castle. She counted the hours and minutes until evening.

Narrator But there was no Beast.

Fearful about his disappearance, Beauty runs crying all through the castle.

Beauty Beast! Where are you? Beast!

Fate 1 She lit a torch and ran into the garden.

Beauty Beast! Beast!

Fate 2 At last, she found him, under a rose bush.

Beauty Motionless, cold, sodden.

Beast I thought I had lost you . . .

Beauty No, Beast! Dear Beast, please don't die. I cannot live without you. Now I know. I love you, Beast. *Ti voglio bene.*

The whole castle bursts into light and is filled with music. Beauty stares in wonder, but when she turns back Beast has gone. At her feet lies a man.

Where is Beast?

Beast You're looking at him. I was cursed by a powerful spell to take the form of a beast. Because I was too proud and arrogant to properly rule my kingdom. The spell could only be broken if an honest and true woman would willingly agree to marry me. There was only you in this whole wide world generous enough to see my repentant heart and be won by it. I offer you my hand and with it my crown.

Beauty Surprised and delighted, she gave her hand to the charming Prince. And together they returned to the castle.

Merchant There she greeted her father.

Sisters But when she turned to her sisters,

Beauty they turned into statues,

Narrator paralysed by jealousy and condemned to stand before their sister's castle gates, watching and watching her happiness.

The Emperor's New Clothes

Weaver 1 The people had an Emperor once, who was so terribly keen on fashion that he spent all his money on fine new clothes.

Weaver 2 He had different clothes for every hour of the day, twenty-four seven, and just as we say of the King that he's in a meeting, it was always said of the Emperor,

Prime Minister I'm sorry, he's in his wardrobe.

Weaver 1 The Emperor lived in the capital city, a vibrant, exciting place. Every day saw new people pouring in.

Weaver 2 One day two swindlers showed up.

Weaver 1 They put it about that they were weavers and could sew the finest garments anyone could imagine.

Weaver 2 The clothes made from their material had the amazing quality of being invisible to anyone who wasn't fit for the position he held or who was well stupid.

Emperor Gosh! They must be wonderful clothes! If I wore them, I'd be able to tell which of my statesmen are unfit for their posts! And I'd be able to sort the clever ones from the thick. Yes! The stuff must be woven for me at once!

Weaver 1 And he paid out a large amount of cash to the swindlers, so that they could start work immediately.

Weaver 2 So they did.

Weaver 1 But there was absolutely nothing on the wheel.

Weaver 2 And nothing in the loom. Zilch.

Emperor Gosh! I wonder how they're getting on with the stuff. I'll send my honest Prime Minister to the weavers. He's the best one to tell what the cloth looks like, for he has brains and no one deserves his position more than him.

Prime Minister So off went the honest Prime Minister to the weavers' workshop. Good heavens above! I can't see anything at all! But he made sure not to say so.

Weaver 1 Come nearer and take a closer look.

Weaver 2 Don't you think the colours and patterns are wonderful?

Prime Minister Crikey! Does this mean that I am stupid? I had no idea! Nobody else had better get wind of it either! Am I unfit for my post? No, I can't possibly admit that I can't see the stuff.

Weaver 2 What d'you think of it, then?

Prime Minister Oh, it's so charming! Quite enchanting! Totally exquisite! What an original pattern! What tasteful colours! Yes, indeed, I like it!

Weaver 1 Oh, we're well pleased to hear that.

Prime Minister And I shall make sure to tell the Emperor how much!

Weaver 2 Now the swindlers demanded more money.

Weaver 1 And they carried on working at the empty frames as before.

Emperor Before too long, the Emperor sent along his sincere Chancellor to see how the weaving was coming along and if the stuff would soon be ready.

Weaver 2 But there was nothing to see.

Weaver 1 Look at that!

Weaver 2 Isn't that a well gorgeous piece of stuff?

Chancellor I know I'm not stupid, so it must be my official position I'm not fit for. Some people would have a good laugh at this, so I must make sure it doesn't get out. Yes, it's fabulous!

Weaver 1 The whole town could talk of nothing else but the wonderful material.

Emperor The Emperor decided that he himself must see it.

Prime Minister Isn't it splendid, Your Imperial Majesty?

Chancellor What colouring! What patterning! If Your Majesty will take a look!

Emperor Gosh! What's going on? I can see nothing at all! This is dreadful! Am I stupid? Am I unfit to be Emperor? This is the most appalling thing that could happen to me . . . Oh, it's so-o-o gorgeous. It has our total approval!

Private Secretaries Oh, it's so-o-o gorgeous!

Prime Minister And then they advised him to have some clothes made from this wonderful new material!

Chancellor And to wear them for the Grand Procession.

Courtier 1 Beautiful!

Courtier 2 To die for!

Weaver 2 Everyone just loved the material!

Emperor The Emperor gave each of them a knighthood, and the title of Imperial Weaver.

Member of Public On the eve of the Grand Procession, the weavers sat up all night by the light of seventeen candles. Everyone could see how hard they were working to finish the Emperor's new clothes. They took the material down from the loom; they snipped and they clipped with huge scissors; and then they sewed busily with needles.

Weaver 1 Sorted!

Weaver 2 The Emperor's new clothes are ready!

Weaver 1 Now, if Your Imperial Majesty will be gracious enough to take off your robe . . .

Weaver 2 Then we will dress you in the new clothes right here.

Weaver 1 Here are the trousers! They are as delicate as gossamer.

Private Secretary 1 What a terrific fit!

Weaver 2 Here is the shirt! As light as a spider's web.

Private Secretary 2 What a pattern!

Weaver 1 And the jacket. You can hardly feel you are wearing anything.

Weaver 2 That's the beauty of them!

Private Secretary 1 It's amazing how well they suit His Majesty!

Private Secretary 2 Yes! Absolutely!

Weavers And here is the long cloak!

Emperor Very well, I am ready. (*Poses in front of mirror.*) Don't they suit me down to the ground?

Private Secretary 1 Wonderful! What colours!

Private Secretary 2 What a gorgeous cloak!

The courtiers, who are to carry the cloak, stoop down and grope about on the floor, as if picking up the cloak. Fanfare.

Prime Minister So the Emperor marched in the Grand Procession.

Chancellor And all the people in the streets were hanging out of the windows.

Private Secretary 1 Look, they said. What a gorgeous cloak!

Private Secretary 2 The Emperor's new clothes are the finest he has ever had, came the cry.

Weaver 1 No one would let anyone else know that he couldn't see anything.

Weaver 2 Because that would have meant he was unfit for his job

Weaver 1 or incredibly stupid.

Emperor Never had the Emperor's clothes been such a howling success!

Child But he's got nothing on!

Prime Minister Good grief!

Chancellor Did you hear what the little thing said?

Private Secretary 1 Stupid child!

Private Secretary 2 His parents should take him home! It's ridiculous!

Weaver 1 But the child's remark was whispered from one person to another. He's got nothing on!

Weavers (*and audience, chanting*) The Emperor is naked! He hasn't got anything on!

Emperor Gosh, well, I must go through with it, procession and all.

Private Secretary 1 And his ministers marched after him,

Private Secretary 2 holding up the cloak that wasn't there.

Weaver 1 Now you've heard the tale

Weaver 2 of the Emperor's new clothes!

Toby and the Wolf

Narrator/Nursemaid A young miller had a dog called Toby.

Wife Toby!

Narrator/Nursemaid The old hound was getting long in the tooth now, and had grown hard of hearing –

Miller TOBY!

Narrator/Nursemaid – so he couldn't guard the house as well as he used to. The miller and his wife neglected Toby, and the servants behaved as their master did. They gave the dog some shoe-leather whenever they passed him and as often as not forgot to feed him.

Toby Toby had such a grim time of it that he made up his mind to turn his back on the mill and chance his luck in the woods.

Narrator/Nursemaid On the way, he bumped into a wolf.

Wolf *Nazdar!* Comrade Toby! Where are you heading?

Toby The dog told him what he had to put up with at the mill and swore he would stick it no longer.

Wolf Brother Toby, you've got plenty of years, but precious little nous. Why leave the mill now, in your old age, and scrape a miserable existence in the woods? Twice, when you were young, you saved the mill from bandits, and now I'm hearing how disgracefully you've been treated! Take a tip from Wolfie and head back to the mill and see to it that the miller feeds you properly.

Toby Comrade Wolf, I would rather die of hunger than crawl back there.

Wolf Dont be so headstrong, Brother Toby. Between us, we'll find the answer to your problems!. Now tomorrow, the nursemaid will come out to the field which the miller is harvesting. True?

Toby True.

Wolf She'll be carrying the miller's baby son. Right?

Toby (*unsure*) Right.

Wolf The moment she puts him down, I'll sneak up and make off with him. Your job is to sniff out my trail and follow it. I will drop the baby in the grass beneath the great oak tree for you to find. Pick him up, take him straight to the miller and he'll greet you like a hero!

Narrtor/Nursemaid The next day, the nursemaid walked out to the field with food for the harvesters, and in one arm she was carrying the miller's baby son. When she reached the field, she laid the baby down on a sheaf and started up joking and flirting with the reapers.

Wolf The wolf crept up, seized the infant, and sped away into the woods.

Narrtor/Nursemaid When the maid saw the wolf running for the trees with the baby in its jaws, she sobbed and screamed for help.

Miller Half out of his mind, the miller ran to fetch his shotgun and hurried to the woods.

Narrator/Nursemaid But he had not gone far before Toby trotted up to the mill, carrying the baby safely in his mouth.

Miller's Wife The miller's wife ordered that Toby be given bread and milk at once.

Miller When the miller came back and was told how Toby had saved his son, he felt so ashamed that he had neglected the old dog that he swore Toby would have nothing but the best from that day forward.

Narrator / Nursemaid And as the tale of the rescue spread, Toby was given a hero's welcome wherever he went.

Wolf One day, the wolf turned up to see Toby as he basked in the sunshine at the back of the mill.

Admit it, Brother, how sound my advice was? You live in the lap of plenty now – so don't forget! One good turn deserves another! I haven't eaten for a week and I need you to help me.

Toby No problem, Brother Wolf. One of the maids is to be married tomorrow and the pantry is stuffed full of meat and pastry and other good scoff for the wedding feast. Let's wait till dark: then we can climb through the window at the back of the pantry and have a feast all of our own!

Narrator / Nursemaid That evening, when darkness fell, the two cronies jumped through the pantry window. They stuffed and supped all night until the wolf became reckless.

Wolf Brother Toby, I'm so happy I feel like a good old sing-song!

Toby You'd better shut up and get out of here quickly or we'll both be discovered and beaten.

Narrator / Nursemaid But the wolf had lost the plot!

The Wolf sings. The Miller is woken.

Miller Filthy thieves!

He thrashes them until the hair flies from their pelts. The Wolf manages to escape but the Miller seizes Toby and chains him up.

Narrator / Nursemaid In the morning,

Miller's Wife the miller's wife begged her husband to let Toby off the chain. The wolf must have led him astray!

Miller (*takes off the chain*) Let this be a warning. Steer clear of the wolf!

Wolf Late one night, the wolf crept into the mill to persuade Toby to take revenge on the miller for the beating.

Toby Toby pointed out that the miller had a big shotgun and could easily shoot them dead.

Wolf Ach, Brother Toby, you're talking like a coward. I'm not going to leave this place with an empty belly. The miller owns a fat old ram. For old times' sake, I want you to drive it out of its pen for me. That way, I can easily kill it and eat my fill without any bother.

Toby Brother Wolf, the ram would be certain to bleat and the miller will come running. You must stand in front of the sheep pen with your mouth open. When I drive the ram out, you must seize him by the head to stop him from bleating and drag him off to the woods sharpish.

Wolf The wolf was all for this and took up position outside the sheep pen.

Toby Toby jumped inside and drove the big, strong ram towards the wolf.

The Ram butts the Wolf, who turns a somersault and crashes down in the yard, unable to move. He groans and wheezes.

Wolf Brother Toby, the ram has knocked the breath out of my body. Keep him away from me!

Hearing the commotion the Miller enters and finds the Ram loose in the yard and the Wolf in front of the sheep pen. He snatches up his shotgun and fires at the Wolf. The Wolf manages to drag himself away.

Narrator / Nursemaid Toby stretched out in his kennel, well pleased at the way matters had turned out.

Toby He told himself that he would never listen to the wolf again.

Wolf But a few days later, what happened but the wolf turned up again. We must make the miller suffer for shooting at me. I have three pellets lodged in my arse. To get even with him, I'm going to destroy his favourite colt.

Toby Toby pleaded with the wolf not to do this, and said that he would have no part in such a revenge.

Wolf I will pin you down and sink my teeth into your scrawny throat if you refuse to help me. Do what I say or you won't move from here alive. Drive the colt out of the stable so that I can fall upon it.

Toby unties the young horse.

Toby (*softly*) Brother Wolf, make sure you bite the back legs first!

The horse kicks out at him with its full strength. The Wolf howls with rage and pain. The Miller hears him, grabs his shotgun and shoots the Wolf dead.

Narrator/Nursemaid Toby gave a great sigh of relief. The wolf could lead him into mischief no more and would never trouble him again. For the rest of his puff, Toby could look forward to living happy ever after in the sunshine.

The Juniper Tree

Narrator/Stonemason Once upon a time, that very old people can still remember,

Father there lived a man and his good and beautiful wife.

Mother They loved each other so much that the only thing they wished for was a little child.

Father Each night before sleep they prayed for a child,

Mother but none came and nothing changed.

Narrator In front of their house grew a juniper tree.

Mother One winter's day, the wife stood under the juniper tree peeling an apple, and as she was peeling it, she cut her finger and her blood wept onto the snow. Oh! (*She sighs deeply.*)

Narrator/Stonemason She grew sad as she looked at the tears of blood on the snow.

Mother If only I had a child as red as blood and as white as snow.

Father These words seemed to lighten her mood.

Mother She felt a glow of cheerfulness as though something might happen.

Narrator/Stonemason After one month, the snow was gone.

Chorus 1 After two months, everything was green.

Chorus 2 After three months, the earth grew flowers.

Chorus 4 After four months, the trees in the forest thickened and their green branches stretched and touched and intertwined.

Chorus 5 The birds began to sing and their songs tumbled from the trees among the falling blossom.

Narrator/Stonemason Soon the fifth month had come and gone and when the wife stood beneath the juniper tree,

Mother its sweet scent flooded her heart with happiness and she fell to her knees, pierced with joy.

Chorus 6 When the sixth month had passed, the fruit was full and swollen and she was serene.

Mother In the seventh month, she picked the juniper berries and ate them so obsessively that she became sick and moody.

Father After the eighth month had passed, she pulled her husband to her and wept.

Mother If I die, bury me under the juniper tree.

Narrator/Stonemason After that, she was calm and contented until the ninth month was over.

Father Then she had a child as red as blood and as white as snow.

Mother But when she looked at her baby for the first time

All she was so ecstatic

Narrator/Stonemason that she died.

Father Her husband buried her under the juniper tree and wept night and day.

Narrator/Stonemason As time passed he began to feel better, but there were still days when he cried. At last he stopped, and after more suns and moons had gone, he found another wife. Together, he and his second wife had a daughter, while his child from his first wife was a little boy, who was as red as blood and as white as snow.

Wife Whenever the woman looked at her daughter, her heart bloomed with love for her. But when she looked at the boy, the same heart jerked. She knew that he would always be there to get in the way of her daughter inheriting everything. Then the devil gripped her until she became very cruel.

She jabs him from here to there, slaps, slippers, clips and cuffs him.

Brother When he came home after school, his life was hell.

Marlene *Mutter*, will you give me an apple?

Wife *Ja, meine liebling.* (*She chooses her the most gorgeous apple from the chest.*)

Marlene *Mutter*, shouldn't Brother have one too?

Wife The woman was annoyed at this. *Ja*, when he gets back from school. And when she looked out of the window and saw the boy coming, the devil tightened his hold on her. No apples until Brother is here.

Marlene leaves as her Brother enters.

Would you like a nice apple, *mein liebling*? (*She gives him a murderous look.*)

Brother Mother, how fierce you look! Yes please, I would like an apple.

Wife Come here, come here. Choose an apple for yourself.

43

*As the boy bends over the chest, the Devil possesses
her, and bang! She slams down the lid so hard that his
little head flies off and rolls among the apples.*

How will I get away with this?

*She balances the boy's head back on his neck and ties
her neckerchief around his throat so that nothing can
be seen. Then she props him up against the chest and
twists an apple into his hand. Marlene enters. Her
mother is in the scullery stirring and stirring a pot of
boiling water.*

Marlene *Mutter.* Brother is sitting by the chest and he
has turned very pale. He's got an apple in his hand, but
when I asked him to give me the apple he wouldn't reply
and now I'm frightened!

Wife Go back to him, and if he still won't answer you,
give him a good clout on the ear.

Marlene Brother, give me the apple.

*She fetches him a box on the ear and his head falls
off. She begins to weep and wail.*

Oh, *Mutter*, I've knocked my brother's head off.

Wife Oh, Marlene, what have you done! You'd better
keep quiet about this. No one must ever know. And
anyway, there's precious little we can do about it now.
We'd best make a stew out of him.

*The Mother chops him into pieces. Then she tosses
them into a pot and lets them simmer and steam and
stew. Marlene stands close by, sobbing, her tears
splashing onto the stew.*

*Father comes home from work and he sits down at
the table.*

Father Where is my son?

The woman dishes up a huge, steamy serving of the stew, and Marlene weeps.

Where's my son?

Wife Oh, he's away to the countryside to visit his mother's great uncle. They'll look after him well.

Father Oh, this has upset me! It's all wrong. He should have said goodbye to me. (*He begins to eat the stew.*) Marlene, what are you blubbing about? Your brother will be home soon enough. Wife, this food is delicious! Dish me up some more! More! Give me some more! I'm not sharing a scrap of it. Somehow I feel this has got my name on it! (*As he chews, he chucks the bones under the table.*)

Marlene (*weeping*) Marlene tenderly gathered up all the bones, tied them up in her silk kerchief and carried them outside. She placed the bones beneath the juniper tree. As she laid them there, she felt suddenly consoled.

Narrator/Stonemason The juniper tree rustled and moved. The branches parted and joined.

Marlene Parted and joined, as though they were clapping their hands with joy.

Narrator/Stonemason Smoke drifted out of the tree. And in the heart of the smoke a fire burned.

Marlene Then a wonderful bird flapped from the flames. He soared higher and higher . . .

Narrator/Stonemason . . . and began to sing.

Bird
Mein mutter she killed me.
Mein vater he ate me.
My sister Marlene made certain to gather
My bones all together,

In silk wrapped so nicely,
Under the juniper tree.
Tweet-tweet!
Under the juniper tree.
Tweet-tweet!
What a beautiful bird I am!

Narrator / Stonemason The bird landed on a roof in the town square.

Goldsmith The goldsmith heard the bird singing and thought the sound was beautiful. He ran from his workshop and didn't stop until he got a good look at the bird. (*He runs outside. He is holding a golden chain.*)

Shoemaker When the shoemaker heard the song, he came hot-footing out onto the street to squinny up at the bird. (*He carries a beautifully crafted pair of red shoes.*)

Stonemason (*chiselling an impossibly heavy millstone*) Then the stonemason chucked chiselling and listened to the words.

Goldsmith Bird, you sing so beautifully!

Shoemaker Sing your song to me again!

Stonemason Let me hear it all!

Bird No, I don't sing twice for nothing.

Goldsmith Take this gold chain!

The bird swoops down and in his right claw he clasps the gold chain.

Shoemaker You see these red shoes? They're yours!

In his left claw he clasps the shoes.

Stonemason But I have nothing to give!

Bird Give me that millstone!

Stonemason If you sing the song again, I'll give you the stone.

The men with effort lift the stone.

Men Heave ho!

The bird pushes his neck through the millstone hole and wears it like a collar.

Bird (*under following narration and dialogue*)
Mein mutter she killed me.
Mein vater he ate me.
My sister Marlene made certain to gather
My bones all together,
In silk wrapped so nicely,
Under the juniper tree.
Tweet-tweet!
Under the juniper tree.
Tweet-tweet!
What a beautiful bird I am!

Narrator/Stonemason As the bird sang he spread his wings. In his right claw, he had the chain, in his left the shoes, and around his neck the millstone. Then he flew away to his father's house.

The Father, the Mother and Marlene are sitting at the table.

Father Hurrah! I'm so happy! I feel absolutely wonderful!

Marlene weeps and weeps throughout the dialogue.

Wife I don't, I don't.

Father Oh, I'm in such a good mood!

Wife I feel scared, as though a huge storm was brewing.

Father I feel just as though I were going to meet an old friend again!

Wife I don't, I don't. My teeth are rattling in my head.

Father The sun is shining at its brightest.

Wife My blood's in flames in my veins.

Bird (*continuing under dialogue but with words clear*) *Mein mutter* she killed me (*etc.*)

The Mother covers her ears and squeezes shut her eyes.

Wife There is a roaring in my head like a huge thunderstorm.

Father Oh, Mother, listen to how beautifully that bird sings.

Wife My eyes are spitting.

Father The sun's so warm,

Wife and it smells of cinnammon.

Father I'm going outside. I have to see this bird close-up.

Wife Don't go! I feel as though the whole house is shaking and ready to burst into flames!

Wife But the man went outside.

The bird drops the golden chain so that it falls neatly around the man's neck.

Father Look how wonderful that bird is! He gave me this gorgeous golden chain.

The woman is petrified and collapses to the floor.

Mother Aah! I wish I was a thousand feet under the earth and did not have to hear this song!

Marlene Oh! I want to go outside as well and see if the bird will give me something too!

The bird throws her the shoes. Marlene slips her feet into the new red shoes and dances back into the house.

Marlene Hurrah! When I went outside I felt so sad, but now I feel full of joy!

Mother I don't, I don't. My hair is flaring like the red flames of hell!

Marlene The bird is so wonderful! He gave me these red shoes as a present!

Wife I feel as if the end of the world is coming! I must get outside!

She rushes outside and is crushed to death by the millstone.

Father The father and Marlene heard the terrible noise and ran outside. Black smoke and red flames were dancing on the spot.

Marlene And when it was finished the little brother stood there alive.

Brother He took hold of his father's hand and Marlene's hand and the three of them were overjoyed.

Narrator/Stonemason They went into the house, sat down at the table, and began to eat.

The Girl and the North Wind

Kari High up in the mountains of Norway a girl lived with her mother.

Mother The girl's name was Kari and one day her mother asked her to fetch the flour to bake loaves and biscuits.

Kari Kari seized the scoop from the kitchen and ran willingly to the barn. She filled the scoop right to the top and hurried back across the yard when – whish-whoosh! – the North Wind swaggered around the corner and scattered all the flour away with one great puff.

Kari went back to the barn, refilled the scoop, and hastened across the yard when – whish-whoosh! – up rushed the North Wind again and blew away all the flour.

She scooped up all the flour that was left, and hugged it to her as she bolted across the yard. But – whish-whoosh! . . .

Mother It'll be gruel for the whole winter now! There'll be no bread and definitely no biscuits till next year!

Kari No biscuits? Well, I'm going to get the flour back! All that day Kari crunched through snow, skirted fjords and trudged up the highest mountains until at last she reached the place where the North Wind lived. North Wind! Come out here! I want to talk to you! Now! North Wind!

North Wind What's all this banging and bawling? How can I have a decent kip with all this commotion?

Kari You stole our flour! You breezed up to our house – *ehn, too, treh* – three times today and blew away all our flour and now we won't have any bread all winter and we'll probably starve to death and it'll be All Your Fault!

North Wind I do apologise. Sometimes I get completely carried away with blowing. I meant no harm, but it's impossible for me to get your flour back now. (*He stares at her for a moment.*) I can't give you your flour back, but I can give you something else. (*handing her a table-cloth*) This cloth is magic. All you have to do is say, 'Cloth, cloth, spread yourself and set out scrumptious scram,' and you will have all the food and drink you can imagine.

Kari Kari thanked the North Wind, and set off home-wards. It was getting dark, but Kari came to an inn on the road and decided to stay the night there.

Troll Hag The inn belonged to a troll hag. *Goo kuelh*.

Kari *Goo kuelh*, good evening.

Inn Regulars *Goo kuelh*.

Kari I was wondering, please may I have a bed for the night?

Troll Hag How will you pay for it?

Kari I am afraid I have no money. But I can feed you and your guests.

Troll Hag How?

Kari Cloth, cloth, spread yourself and set out scrumptious scram! At once the cloth was groaning with food –

Regular 1 soups and soufflés,

Regular 2 roasts and stews,

51

Regular 3 steaks and sausages,

Regular 4 pies and flans,

Troll Hag trifles and puddings,

Kari and every kind of drink.

Regular 1 Aquavit,

Regular 2 wine,

Regular 3 beer,

Regular 4 chocolate,

Troll Hag tea.

Kari When all the guests at the inn had filled their boots, Kari rolled up her cloth and went to bed.

Troll Hag But at dead of night, when everyone was in the land of nod, the troll crone came creeping up the stairs with a cloth identical to Kari's. She sneaked into her room and swapped her cloth for hers.

Kari Next morning, Kari snatched the cloth and sprinted all the way home. Mam! Mam! Look what the North Wind gave me. Cloth, cloth, spread yourself and set out scrumptious scram! Nothing! Cloth, cloth, spread yourself and set out scrumptious scram. (*desperately*) Cloth, cloth, spread yourself and set out stupid scram!

Mother What's the good in twisting the cloth this way and that?

Kari The North Wind has tricked me! Kari marched off to the North Wind's house before her mother could say no. North Wind! Come outside! I want to talk to you!.

North Wind You again? (*yawning*) Why are you back so soon?

Kari You know very well why I'm back! The cloth you gave me was useless! It only worked once and what good is that?

North Wind Just the once? Something is wrong. But let's not quarrel. I'll give you something else. This goat is magic. All you have to do is say, 'Goat! Splosh! Crip, crap, dosh!' and it will make all the money you need!

Kari Will it work more than once?

North Wind For ever.

Kari So Kari took the goat and set off homewards, returning to the inn for the night. *Goo kuelh*, good evening, I was wondering if I could have a bed for tonight?

Troll Hag How are you going to pay?

Kari Goat! Splosh! Crip, crap, dosh! Immediately, out of its backside, dropped a jackpot of gold coins. Kari paid the crone, and then went to bed.

Troll Hag In the middle of the night, the troll crone once more came crawling up the stairs, this time with her own goat, which she switched for Kari's.

Kari When Kari got home next day, she showed her mother just what the goat could do.

Mother An old goat?

Kari Goat! Splosh! Crip, crap, dosh!

Mother Whatever is coming out of that goat's rear end, certainly isn't gold!

Kari Kari stomped back to the North Wind, more livid than ever.

North Wind Something is wrong. I'll give you one last thing, but you'd better use it wisely. This stick is magic. All you have to do is say 'Stick, stick, lay on!' and it will thrash anyone you want. When you want it to stop, just say 'Stick, stick, lay off!' and it will come straight back to you.

Kari Kari thanked the North Wind and went straight to the inn.

Troll Hag *and* **Regulars** *Goo kuelh!*

Kari May I have a bed for the night?

Troll Hag How do you plan to pay?

Kari finds some spare coins in her apron.

In the dark small hours, the crone came creeping up the stairs again, certain the stick was magic.

Kari Stick, stick, lay on!

The stick gives the troll crone a hiding.

Troll Hag Make it stop! Make it stop!

Kari Not until you give me back my cloth and my goat!

Troll Hag I will, I will!

Kari Stick, stick, lay off! At once the stick flew – whish-whoosh – into her hand. But she kept a firm grip of it as she marched behind the troll crone to fetch her cloth and her goat.

The next morning, Kari ran home with her treasures. Cloth, cloth spread yourself and set out scrumptious scram! Goat, splosh, crip, crap, dosh! And with them she and her mother had all the food and money and protection they needed

Mother *and* **Kari** for the rest of their long and extremely happy lives.

Company
Snipp, snapp, snute,
Her er eventyret ute!
Snip, snap snut,
My gob's now shut!

Beasts and Beauties

EIGHT TALES FROM EUROPE

Retold by Carol Ann Duffy

Blue Beard

Once upon a time, there lived a man who owned many splendid properties in the town and in the country, who possessed an abundance of silver and gold plate, handcrafted furniture, the finest porcelain and glass, and coaches trimmed all over with gold. But he was the owner of something else as well – a blue beard which made him so appallingly ugly that women and girls took one look at him and fled.

He had a neighbour, a society lady, who had two fine sons and two daughters who were flowers of beauty. He asked her for one of the girls' hand n marriage and told her she could choose herself which one of them she would give to him as bride. Neither of the girls would have him, though, and they sent him backwards and forwards, up, down and sideways from one to the other, both adamant they would not marry a man with a blue beard. But there was something else which repelled them even more and filled them with fear and revulsion. He had already been married to several wives and no one living knew what had happened to them.

Blue Beard, to try and win the girls over, escorted them with my lady, their mama, and three or four other mademoiselles of quality, and some fine young people of the district, to one of his country estates, where they were entertained for eight sumptuous days. So now it was all parties and candles and music and masks; it was hunting and shooting and fishing; it was dancing and feasting and the finest champagne and armagnac. It was *merci, monsieur* and *enchanté*, and *oooh la la*! In fact, everything went so splendidly, that the youngest daughter started to think that the lord of the manor's beard wasn't actually *bleu, mais non*, not really, and that he was a most civilised gentleman.

No sooner were they home than the marriage was held. A month after that, Blue Beard told his wife that he had to travel to a distant country for at least six weeks, on a matter of extreme importance. He encouraged her to amuse herself while he was away. She was to send for her friends and family, go to the countryside if she wished, and generally have a good time wherever she went. Here, he said, are the keys to the two Great Rooms that contain my best and most costly furniture; these grant access to my silver and gold plate, which is to be used sparingly; these open my strong chests, which hold all my money; these my casket of jewels; and this here is the master key that opens all my apartments. But this little one here is the key to the closet at the far end of the great gallery. Open everything and go anywhere, but do not unlock the little closet. I forbid you this – and I want you to know that I forbid you so solemnly that if you disobey me, you can seek no hiding place from my fury. She promised to do everything just as he said and so he squeezed her to him, then climbed into his coach and began his journey.

Her friends and family didn't wait to be invited – they were so impatient to see all the splendour of the newlyweds' house. Only her brothers didn't come because their military duties delayed them. But all the others rushed straight to the two great rooms, flinging wide all the closets and wardrobes to gape and coo at the finery, which got more splendid with every door they opened. They could not say enough about their envy and delight at their friend's good fortune. She, however, paid not the slightest attention to all the treasures, because she was burning up with curiosity about the little closet. She became so consumed by this, that without even thinking how rude it was to abandon her guests, she rushed down the back stairs so recklessly that she could have broken her slender neck three times over.

60

When she reached the closet door, she hesitated for quite a while, remembering her husband's warnings, and worrying about the consequences if she disobeyed him. But temptation was far too strong for her and she could not resist it. She picked out the little key and opened the door, shaking all over. At first, she could make out nothing clearly at all, because the shutters were all closed. But after a few moments she saw that the floor was spattered with lumps of congealed blood, and upon it lay the bodies of several dead women, each sprawled there, or hanging in her wedding gown. These were the brides that Blue Beard had married and had slaughtered one after another. She nearly died of terror and as she jerked the key from the lock it fell from her hand. She tried to calm herself, picked up the key, locked the door, and hurried up the stairs to her chamber to try to recover. But she was too frightened. Then she noticed that the key to the closet was stained with blood, so she tried three times to scrub it off, but the blood would not come off even though she scoured it with soap and sand. The key was magic, and when she rubbed the blood from one side it would appear again on the other. That evening, when her guests said their *au revoirs*, she begged her sister to remain.

Unexpectedly, Blue Beard interrupted his journey and came home, saying that he had received a message on the road that the important business he was on his way to deal with was completed to his satisfaction. His wife did everything to act as though she was delighted by his sudden return. The next morning he asked her for the keys, but her hand shook so violently as she gave them to him that he guessed at once what had happened. Why is it, he said, that the key to the closet is missing? Oh! I must have left it upstairs on the table, she said. Make sure, said Blue Beard, that you fetch it to me shortly; and after going backwards and forwards several times, she was forced to bring him the key. Blue Beard turned the key over and over, looking at it very carefully, then said to his wife, How did this blood get on the key? I don't know, answered the poor girl, white as a dead bride. You don't know, said Blue Beard, you don't know; but *I* know. You were determined to go into the closet, weren't you? Very well, madame, you shall go in and take your place among the sisterhood you found there.

At this, she flung herself at her husband's feet and pleaded pitifully for his forgiveness, swearing that she was sorry and would never disobey him again. Even a stone would have been moved by her beauty and grief, but Blue Beard's heart was harder than any stone. You must die, *chérie*, he said, and soon. If I have to die, she said through her tears, then allow me a little time to dress in my bridal shroud. You may have a quarter of an hour, said Blue Beard, but not a second longer.

As soon as she was alone, she called to her sister and said, Sister, I need you to climb up to the top of the tower and see if my brothers are coming. They promised me they would come here today, so if you see them then give them a signal to hurry. Her sister went up to the top of the tower, and the terrified woman cried out, Sister, Sister, do you see anything coming? And her sister replied, I see nothing but the sun making dust and the grass growing green. Meanwhile, Blue Beard was sharpening and sharpening a huge knife, and chanting horribly:

Sharper, sharper, shiny knife,
Cut the throat of whiny wife!

Then he shouted out, Come down at once or I'll come up to you! Just one moment longer, please, said his wife, first I have to fasten my corsage and pull on my silken stockings; and then she called up very softly, Sister, Sister, do you see anything coming? And her sister said, I see nothing but the sun and the dust and the grass. Blue Beard was sharpening and chanting even more ferociously:

Sharper, sharper, knife so dear,
Slit her throat from ear to ear!

Get down here now! he bawled, or I'll come up to you. I'm coming, said his wife, I just have to tie my garter and slip on my shoes, and then she cried out, Sister, Sister, do you see anything coming? I see, answered her sister, a great dust rolling in on this side here. *Is it my brothers?* Oh, no, my dear sister! It's just a flock of sheep. Blue Beard sharpened and chanted even more vigorously:

Now the knife is sharp enough,
And ready for the bloody stuff!

Come down here now! he bellowed, or I'll be up for you! One last moment, said his wife, I have only my veil to secure and my white kid gloves. Then she cried, Sister, Sister, do you see anything coming? I can see, she said, two horsemen coming, but they are still a long way off. Thanks be to God, she cried at once, it is our brothers! I have made them a sign to make great haste. Blue Beard roared out now so loudly that the whole house shook.

The poor woman came down and collapsed at his feet, with her face jewelled with tears and her hair loose about her shoulders. This won't help, said Blue Beard, you must die; then, grasping her hair with one hand and raising the cutlass with the other, he was about to cut off her head. His wife writhed around and, looking at him with dying eyes, begged him for one last moment to collect herself. No, no, no, he said, give yourself over to God! At this exact moment there came such a thunderous knocking at the gates that Blue Beard froze. The gates were opened and immediately the two horsemen entered. They saw Blue Beard, drew their swords and rushed straight at him. He saw that they were the brothers of his wife – one a dragoon and the other a musketeer – so he ran for his life. But the

63

brothers were too fast for him and caught him before he even reached the steps to the porch. Then they ran their swords through his body and left him there dead.

Their poor sister was scarcely more alive than her husband and was too weak to stand and embrace her brothers. Blue Beard had no heirs and so his wife became owner of all his estate. With one part, she gave a dowry to her sister, to marry a young gentleman who had loved her truly for a long time; another part she spent to buy captains' commissions for her brothers; and she used the rest to marry herself to a very kind gentleman, who soon made her forget the dark time she had spent with Blue Beard.

The Husband Who Was to Mind
the House for the Day

A man once stomped about northern parts who was so grumpy and surly that he thought his wife could do nowt right in the house. So one evening, during harvest time, he came cursing, blowing and fuming home, showing his teeth and kicking up a right dust.

'My love, you mustn't be so angry,' said his goody. 'Tomorrow why don't we swap our work? I'll go out with the mowers and mow, and you can keep house at home.'

Aye, the husband thought, that would do nicely. He was agreeable to that, he said.

So, first thing next morning, his goody put the scythe over her neck and walked out into the hayfield with the mowers and set off mowing. And the man was to stop at home, mind the house, and do the housework.

His first task was to churn the butter, but when he had churned for a bit, he worked up a thirst, and went down to the cellar to tap a barrel of ale. But just when he had knocked in the bung and was fitting the tap to the cask, above his head he heard the pig lumber into the kitchen. So off he legged it up the cellar steps, the tap in his fist, as fast as he could, to sort out the pig before it knocked over the churn. But the pig had already knocked over the churn, and stood there, snuffling and rooting in the cream which was pouring all over the floor. The husband became so mad with rage that he forgot about the ale barrel and charged at the pig as hard as he could. He caught it as well, just as it squealed through the door, and landed it such a kick that poor piggy lay for dead on the ground. Then he remembered he had the tap in his hand; but when

65

he ran down to the cellar, every last drop of ale had drip-ped out of the cask.

So he went into the dairy and found enough leftover cream to fill the churn again, and he started up churning once more, for there'd better be butter at dinner. After he'd churned for a while, he remembered that their milk-ing cow was still locked up in the cowshed and hadn't been fed or watered all morning, even though the sun was rid-ing high in the sky. But then he thought it was too far to lead her down to the meadow, so he'd just put her up on the top of the house. The house, you should realise, had a roof which was thatched with sods and a thick crop of grass had sprouted up there. The house was built close to a steep slope and he reckoned that if he laid a plank across to the thatch at the back, he'd get the cow up no problem.

But he still couldn't leave the churn because there was his baby crawling around on the floor and, 'If I leave it,' he thought, 'the child is sure to knock it over.' So he heaved the churn onto his back and went off out; but then he thought he'd best water the cow before he put her up on the thatch; so he picked up a bucket to draw water from the well but, as he bent over the mouth of the well, all the cream poured out of the churn over his shoulders and vanished into the well. Then he gave the cow some water and put her up on the thatch.

It was getting near dinner-time and he hadn't even sorted the butter yet, so he decided he'd better boil up the porridge, so he filled the pot with water and hung it over the fire. When he'd done that, he worried that the cow might fall off the roof and break her neck or her legs, so he climbed onto the roof to tie her up. He tied one end of the rope round the cow's neck and made it fast, and the other end he slid down the chimney and tied it round his own thigh. And he had to get a move on, because the water was bubbling in the pot and he hadn't even begun grinding the oatmeal yet.

So he started to grind away; but while he was going at it hammer and tongs, the cow fell off the top of the house anyway, and as she fell, she dragged the man up the chimney by his leg. He was stuck there like a cork in a bottle and the cow hung halfway down the wall, dangling between heaven and earth, unable to get either up or down.

Meanwhile, the goody had been waiting seven lengths and seven widths of the field for her husband to call her to dinner, but no call came. Finally, she reckoned she'd worked and waited long enough, so she went home. The moment she got there she saw the ugly sight of the cow swinging on the wall, so she ran up and cut the rope in two with her scythe. As soon as she did this, her husband came crashing down out of the chimney; and so, when his old dame came into the kitchen, there she found her baby cradling the half-dead pig and her husband standing on his brainbox in the porridge pot. This is what happened the day the husband was to mind the house.

The Three Wishes

It was a very long time ago, and it was once, that a poor woodman dwelled in a great English forest. Every day that he lived, out he went to fell timber. One fine day, off he went and the wood-wife packed his pouch and looped his bottle over his shoulder and under his armpit, and that was his meat and drink for the forest. He had his eye on a huge old oak, reckoning it would yield strong planks aplenty. When he stood beneath it, out came his axe and around his bonce it swung as though he was trying to deck the oak with a stroke. But he hadn't landed so much as a blow when his ears heard pitiful plaintive pleas and he clapped eyes on a fairy, who begged and beseeched him to spare the tree. He was stunned – you can imagine – with fascination and fear, and he couldn't force one word through his lips. At last he found his tongue. 'Well,' he said, 'I'll do as thou wants.'

'You have done yourself a greater favour than you know,' replied the fairy, 'and I propose to show my gratitude by granting you your next three wishes, whatever they may be.' At that, the fairy was nowhere to be seen and the woodman hung his pouch over his shoulder and slung his bottle at his side and loped for home.

Well, the way was a long one and the poor man was flummoxed and flabbergasted by the magical thing that had happened to him, and when he got home there was nowt in his noddle but a strong desire to sit in his chair and rest. Perhaps this was the work of the fairy? Your guess. Anyroad, he plonked himself down next to the toasty fire and as he sat he grew hungry, even though it was a long time till supper.

'Has thou owt for supper, wife?' he called to the wood-wife.

'Nowt for a couple of hours yet,' she said.

'Aah!' groaned the woodman. 'I wish I had a long strong link of black pudding in front of my face!'

No sooner had the words left his lips when bonk, slither, clatter and clunk, what should fall down the chimney but a long strong link of the finest black pudding a man's belly could desire.

If the woodman gaped, the wood-wife gawped to the power of three. 'What's happened here?' she said.

Then the woodman remembered the morning's events and he told his story from start to finish, and as he told it the wood-wife glowered and glared, and when he'd finished she exploded, 'Thou fool! Thou fool! Thou fool! I wish the pudding was on your nose, I really do!'

And before you could say Flingo Macbingo, there the good man sat and his neb was longer by a noble length of black pudding.

He gave a tug, but it stuck, and she gave a yank, but it stuck, then they both pulled till they nearly tore off his nose, but it stuck and it stuck and it stuck.

'What's to happen now?' he said.

'It doesn't look *that* bad,' she said, giving him a good looking over.

Then the woodman realised that he must wish and wish quick; so wish he did and his wish was for the black pudding to be off his conk. Alleluia! There it gleamed in a dish on the table, and if the woodman and wood-wife never rode in a fairy-tale coach or danced in satin and silk, well, at least they had as splendid a link of long strong black pudding as ever the heart and stomach of a man or a woman could wish for.

Beauty and the Beast

Once upon a time, there was a rich merchant who had three daughters. The girls were just as clever as they were *bella* and none more so than the youngest, whose name was Beauty. Her sisters were jealous of her. They swanned about going to parties and pageants and jeered at Beauty because she liked to stay at home with her books. Many suitors came to court the three girls. The two eldest trilled that they would consider betrothal to nothing below a count, so there! Beauty, in her turn, gently thanked the eligible young men but chose to remain in her father's house for a while yet.

One dark day, the merchant lost all his fortune. Only the tears in his eyes were silver as he told his daughters that his wealth was gone. They must all move at once to the country and work for their living. This was a dreadful shock to the girls, who had never lifted a dainty finger in their lives. Beauty got up at first light to cook, clean, make, mend, tidy, scour and scrub. But she made sure she read her books too, and in less than a couple of months she was fitter and bonnier than ever. Her two sisters, however, did nothing but whine and whinge about the loss of their fine frocks and fancy friends. 'And look at her,' they moaned one to the other, 'how snide she is to be happy with such an awful life!' But Beauty's father was proud of his hard-working, modest daughter.

A grim year passed, then one morning the merchant received news of the safe arrival of one of his ships that had been thought lost. The two eldest girls were in raptures and demanded a wardrobe of expensive dresses so they could shimmy back to society in high style. Beauty privately thought that their father's money would hardly stretch to one gown each, but rather than seem to be critical of her sisters' eager pestering she asked for a rose.

The Merchant set off to reclaim his cargo, but there were debts to be paid and legal matters to settle and, after a bundle of trouble, he had to head for home as penniless as before. As he returned through the Great Forest, a blinding snowstorm, like a frenzy of torn-up paper money, raged around him and he lost his way. It was foolhardy to struggle on through the icy blizzard, but he knew if he stayed put he would freeze to death and already he could hear the bloodthirsty howling of wolves who had sniffed him out. Exhausted and on the lip of despair, he saw – thank God! – a light in the distance and ran, ran for his life, until he reached a magnificent castle.

The doors were open. In he went to make himself known but there was no reply to his hellos. Only the fire spat and crackled and he saw that the table was sumptuously laid for one. 'I hope the master here or his servants will forgive this intrusion!' He waited and waited until it looked like all the good food and wine would be wasted, so he sat down nervously and began to eat and drink. He ate with jittery gusto and after a glass of vino or four he plucked up the courage to explore the castle. He came to a room with the softest, plumpest of beds in it. He lay down, tired to his bones, and fell fast asleep.

It was late next morning when he was awakened by the rich scent of hot chocolate and sweet biscotti. He sniffed gratefully! 'This castle must belong to a kind spirit who has taken pity on me! *Grazzi*, dear good spirit!' Outside, instead of snow, was the most beautiful rose garden anyone with eyes under his eyebrows had ever seen. Recalling Beauty's request, he stepped outside to pick her a rose. The sweet, heady perfume of an opening red rose drew him towards it, but as he snapped its stem he was nearly deafened by the horrifying roar of some kind of beast charging at him.

'Ungrateful man!' thundered the creature. 'I have saved

71

your life by letting you into my castle and to thank me you steal one of my roses which I prize over everything! You have one quarter of an hour before you meet death!'

The merchant fell to his knees and raised up his hands.

'My Lord, I beg you to pardon me! Believe me, I didn't know I would offend you by picking a rose for my youngest daughter!'

'My name is not My Lord,' snarled the beast, 'Don't flatter me. My name is Beast. You say you have daughters. I will spare your life on one condition – that one of them comes here of her own free will and suffers for your sake. Swear that if none of your daughters offers to die in your place you will return here within three months.'

The merchant had no intention of sacrificing one of his girls, but he thought that by agreeing to the bargain he could at least say a proper goodbye to them. He swore on oath to return and then he left the castle with as much despair as he had entered it with relief.

By the time the moon was up, the good man was home. His daughters ran to meet him but instead of hugging them happily, he held out the rose and wept.

'Take it, Beauty,' he sobbed, 'though you cannot imagine the price I must pay for it.'

Then he told them his terrible tale. At once, her elder sisters rounded on Beauty viciously. So much for her pride! She couldn't just ask for pretty dresses like they did. Oh no! Miss Goody Two-Shoes had to *distinguish* her stuck-up saintly self and now she would be the *death* of their poor father. And look at her! Completely dry-eyed! How *callous*! How *heartless*!

'Why should I shed any tears?' said Beauty. 'If the monster will take any one of us three then I will volunteer to quench his fury. Earning my father his life will prove my love for him.'

'Don't even think of it,' cried the merchant. 'I am old and my life is nearly done. I cannot accept this precious gift.'

But Beauty would not be dissuaded and he had to agree. Her two sisters were well pleased because Beauty's goodness drove them crazy and they were glad to be shot of her. And when the day came for Beauty to leave, they had to scrub at each other's hard eyes with an onion to squeeze out a few tears.

The merchant and his youngest child journeyed to the castle and discovered in the great hall there a table plentifully laid for two. 'The Beast wants to fatten me up before he devours me,' thought Beauty. At last the Beast stood before them and Beauty recoiled at his sickening appearance, but promised she had come of her own free will.

'You are good,' said the Beast, 'and I appreciate this, honest man. Get on your way now and take this chest of gold to buy costly silks for your other daughters. Don't ever think of returning here.'

The Beast vanished as suddenly as he'd appeared.

'Oh, Beauty,' croaked the merchant, 'I am scared half out of my wits for you. Let me be the one to stay!'

'No,' said Beauty firmly and to comfort her father she smiled warmly and hugged him. But the wretched man cried bitterly when he left his beloved child.

Now the poor girl was all alone for her last few hours. She wandered through the fine castle, noticing every charming thing. Before long she came to a door above which was written her own name. Inside was a wonderful collection of books that made her gasp with pleasure. Her eye fell on a book of gold. Inside was written:

Welcome, Beauty. Have no fear.
You are Queen and govern here.
Say your heart's desires aloud,
Your secret wishes. Don't be proud.

'My only wish is to see my father.'

No sooner had the words left her lips than she noticed a mirror and was amazed to see within it her father arriving

73

home, safe but almost broken with grief. Her sisters were pretending to share his sorrow but they could barely keep the satisfaction of getting rid of Beauty off their faces. A moment later the image faded and was gone.

That night Beauty was treated to a splendid musical concert, but she didn't see a soul. Despite everything, she felt strangely at peace and drifted out into the garden to luxuriate in the perfumes of her favourite flowers. A gross and hideous noise made her jump and she couldn't stop herself exclaiming with shock as she found herself staring straight into the hot, ravenous eyes of Beast. Blood dripped from his teeth and in his jaws was the raw flesh of a fresh-killed animal. Beauty froze. Beast's naked shape cringed in unspeakable shame and a heartstopping wail filled the night as he fled.

Beauty could not remember how she had got to her bedchamber that night. When she awoke in the morning she thought the whole frightful incident had been a nightmare. But there was a note on her pillow which read: 'From now on you shall walk in the gardens undisturbed.'

The next night at supper, to Beauty's horror, Beast was there, dressed in his best velvet *capa*. He was courteous and polite and Beauty noticed that he tried his best to display excellent table manners. But the noises he made when he ate disgusted her and she couldn't hide this. Beast hung his head and said:

'Forgive me, Beauty.'

She could tell he meant it and she swallowed hard and nodded. But Beast saw that she hadn't touched her food and said: 'If my presence distresses you, I will leave at once. Do I revolt you?'

'I cannot lie. You do. But I know you are very . . . good-natured.'

'Yes. Even so, I am a monster.'

'There are plenty who deserve that name more than you do. I prefer you to someone who conceals a twisted heart behind an upright form.'

74

'I am grateful to you.' After a pause the Beast continued, 'Beauty? Will you consent to be my wife?'

Beauty gagged at these words and it was some time before she summoned the nerve to answer him. But at last she said shaking, 'No, Beast.'

The poor monster hissed dreadfully, like a thousand snakes, and the whole castle echoed. He withdrew at once, leaving Beauty to suffer a tangled knot of revulsion and compassion.

Time passed. Compassion grew like a rose and the weed of revulsion withered. Beauty had spent three contented months in the castle. Each evening Beast came to her and they were good companions, talking, reading or listening to music. She had grown used to his grotesque features and eating problems and instead of dreading his visits would find herself looking at the clock to check when he was coming. Only one thing troubled her. Every night before she retired, the monster asked if she would be his wife. One evening she said to him:

'Beast, your question makes me anxious. I wish I could agree to marry you, but I can't. I shall always be fond of you as a friend. Please try to be happy with that.'

'I ought to be happy as we are because I know how badly I'm afflicted. I value friendship, too, but I love you, Beauty, deeply and tenderly. Promise me this: you will never leave me.'

Beauty coloured and answered truthfully that she promised never to leave him. Then she added: 'But if I don't see my father again, I shall *never* be happy.'

'I would rather die than make you unhappy.'

'I swear to you that I will return in one week.'

'Then you shall be there in the morning,' said Beast. 'When you want to come back to me, lay this ring on a table before you fall asleep. *Arrivederci*, Beauty.'

When she awoke the next day, Beauty was in her father's house, which was still out in the country despite the gold

75

that Beast had given. The good man thought he would die of shock and happiness when he saw his treasured Beauty again. He summoned her two sisters, who had moved to town with their new husbands. They were both deeply unhappy. The eldest had married a gorgeous gentleman, but he fancied himself so much he never looked at her. The second had wed a man famed for his wit, but he only used it now to torment and torture his wife.

Beauty's sisters nearly fell down with envy when they saw her dressed as a princess and glowing radiantly.

'Sister,' hissed the eldest, 'I have an idea. Let's try to keep Miss Perfect here for more than a week and, who knows, the stupid monster will be so angry she didn't keep her promise that he'll eat her.'

'Excellent,' agreed the other. 'We must show her as much kindness as we can.'

They managed this so well that their younger sister was truly touched and when the week was over she was easily won over by their tears and entreaties.

So the family enjoyed more precious days together, but as each one passed Beauty felt more and more anxious about deserting Beast. It wasn't just that she'd broken her promise – she longed to see him again. She caught herself thinking about his kind heart and his thoughtfulness. She remembered the desolate look in his eyes when she turned down his offer of marriage. She was sorry he was so hideous, but she thought, 'It's not his fault. And I know I'd be much happier with him than my sisters are with their husbands. I might not love him in the way that he loves me, but we are good friends. I can't stand making him so unhappy.'

So she put her ring on the table and went to bed.

When she awoke the next morning she realised that she felt true joy at being back in Beast's castle. She dressed in her loveliest gown and counted the hours and minutes until evening. But the castle held only silence and there was no

Beast. Fearful about his disappearance and distraught that she might be the cause of it, Beauty ran weeping and crying all through the castle. Beast was nowhere. She lit a torch and ran into the garden, desperately calling his name.

At last, she found him, motionless, cold, sodden, under a rose bush. Beauty flung herself upon him, afraid he was dead, and pressed her heart to his as her tears blessed his face. 'I thought I had lost you,' gasped Beast, 'but now I am seeing you for the last time, I can die happy.'

'No, Beast!' sobbed Beauty. 'My dear, dear Beast, please don't die. This terrible grief I feel tells me that I cannot live without you. I thought we could only be friends but now I know . . . I love you, Beast. *Ti voglio bene*.'

As Beauty uttered these words the whole castle burst into light and was filled with sweet music. Beauty stared in wonder but when she turned back to Beast he was gone. At her feet lay a man. Although he was handsome and well-made, she asked anxiously, 'Where is Beast?'

'You're looking at him,' he smiled. 'Let me explain. Because I was too proud and arrogant to properly rule my kingdom, I was cursed by a powerful spell to take the form of a beast. The spell could only be broken if an honest and true woman would willingly agree to marry me. There was only you in this whole wide world generous enough see my repentant heart and be won by it. I offer you my hand and with it my crown.'

Beauty, surprised and delighted, gave her hand to the charming Prince and together they returned to the castle. Her family had been taken there and she ran to her father's arms. But when she turned to her sisters, they turned into statues, paralysed by jealousy and condemned to stand before their sister's castle gates, watching and watching her happiness.

The Emperor's New Clothes

The people had an Emperor once, who was so terribly keen on fashion that he spent all his money on fine new clothes. He took absolutely no interest in his army, or going to the theatre, and would only drive through the country in order to show off his latest outfit. He had different clothes for every hour of the day, twenty-four seven, and just as we say of the King that he's in a meeting, it was always said of the Emperor, 'He's in his wardrobe.'

The Emperor lived in the capital city, a vibrant, exciting place. Every day saw new people pouring in, and one day two swindlers showed up. They put it about that they were weavers and could weave the finest garments anyone could imagine. Not only were their colours and designs incredibly attractive, but the clothes made from their material had the amazing quality of being invisible to anyone who wasn't fit for the position he held or who was well stupid.

'Gosh! They must be wonderful clothes,' thought the Emperor. 'If I wore them, I'd be able to tell which of my statesmen are unfit for their posts! And I'd be able to sort the clever ones from the thick. Yes! The stuff must be woven for me at once!' And he arranged for a large amount of cash to be paid to the swindlers, so that they could start work immediately.

So they did: they set up a couple of looms and pretended to be weaving away, but there was absolutely nothing in the looms. Nowt. Zilch. Cool as you like, they demanded the most delicate silk and the finest gold thread, which they promptly stashed in their own pockets; and then they went on weaving nothing far into the small hours at their empty looms.

'Gosh! I wonder how they're getting on with the stuff,' said the Emperor to himself. But there was one thing that was really worrying him – and this was that a man who was stupid or quite unfit for his position would never be able to see what had been woven. Not that he had anything to fear on his own account, not at all, not at all, but, all the same, it was probably sensible to send along somebody else first to see how things were coming along. The whole city had heard of the strange power possessed by the material and everyone was desperate to find out how crap or daft their neighbours were.

'I'll send my honest Prime Minister to the weavers,' thought the Emperor. 'He's the best one to tell what the cloth looks like, for he has brains and no one deserves his position more than him.'

So off went the honest Prime Minister to the workshop where the two swindlers sat cheating at their empty looms.

'Good heavens above!' thought the Prime Minister, with his eyes popping out of his head. 'I can't see anything at all!' But he made sure not to say so.

The two swindlers begged him to come nearer and take a closer look. Didn't he think their colours and patterns were wonderful? Then they pointed to their empty looms and although the poor Prime Minister widened and widened his eyes, he couldn't see a thing because there wasn't a thing to see. 'Crikey!' he thought. 'Does this mean that I am stupid? I had no idea! Nobody else had better get wind of it either! Am I unfit for my post? No, I can't possibly admit that I can't see the stuff.'

'What d'you think of it then?' asked one of the weavers.

'Oh, it's so charming! Quite enchanting! Totally exquisite!' said the poor Prime Minister, staring through his spectacles. 'What an original pattern! What tasteful colours! Yes, indeed, I shall make sure to tell the Emperor how much I like it!'

'Oh, we're well pleased to hear that,' said the swindlers,

and then they named all the colours and described the unusual design. The Prime Minister listened carefully, so he could repeat it all to the Emperor – which he did.

Now the swindlers demanded more money, more fine silk and more gold thread, which they said was needed for weaving. But it all went straight into their own pockets – not one thread went onto the loom – and they carried on working at the empty frames as before.

Before too long, the Emperor sent along another sincere statesman to see how the weaving was coming along and if the stuff would soon be ready. Just like the Prime Minister, he looked and looked, but, as there was nothing there, there was nothing to see.

'Look at that! Isn't that a well gorgeous piece of stuff?' said the swindlers, and they drew his attention to the prettiness of the design which wasn't there at all.

'I know I'm not stupid,' thought the man, 'so it must be my official position I'm not fit for. Some people would have a good laugh at this, so I must make sure it doesn't get out.' So he praised the material which he could not see and complimented them on its beautiful colours and charming design. 'Yes, it's fabulous!' he said to the Emperor when he got back.

The whole town could talk of nothing else but the wonderful material. The Emperor decided that he himself must see it while it was still on the loom. With a crowd of hand-picked courtiers, including the two esteemed officials who had already visited, the Emperor arrived at the workshop. Both crafty villains were weaving away like the clappers without so much as a thread between them.

'Isn't it splendid, Your Imperial Majesty?' said the two honest statesmen. 'What colouring! What patterning! If Your Majesty will take a look!' And they pointed to the empty looms, quite sure that everyone else could see the stuff.

'Gosh! What's going on?' thought the Emperor. 'I can see nothing at all! This is dreadful! Am I stupid? Am I unfit to be Emperor? This is the most appalling thing that could happen to me . . . Oh, it's so-o-o gorgeous,' he said to them. 'It has our total approval!' And he nodded his head up and down contentedly as he gazed at the empty loom. After all, he wasn't going to say that he couldn't see a thing. The crowd of courtiers who had come with him looked and looked, but they could see no more than anyone else had done. But they all copied the Emperor and said, 'Oh, it's so-o-o gorgeous!' And then they advised him to have some clothes made from this wonderful new material and to wear them for the Grand Procession that was soon to take place. 'Beautiful!' 'Divine!' 'Superb!' 'To die for!' were the compliments that scurried from mouth to mouth. Everyone just *loved* the material and the Emperor gave each of the swindlers a knighthood, with a badge for his buttonhole, and the title of Imperial Weaver.

On the eve of the Grand Procession, the swindlers sat up all night by the light of seventeen candles. Everyone could see how hard they were working to finish the Emperor's new clothes. They pretended to take the material down from the loom; they snipped and they clipped at the air with huge scissors; they sewed busily with needles that had no thread in them, and at the end of it all they said, 'Sorted! The Emperor's new clothes are ready!'

Then the Emperor himself arrived, surrounded by all his statesmen; and the two swindlers held out their arms, as though they were displaying the new clothes, and said, 'Here are the trousers! Here is the jacket! Here is the long cloak!' And so on. 'They are as delicate as gossamer, as light as a spider's web; you can hardly feel you are wearing anything – that's the beauty of them!'

'Yes! Absolutely!' chorused all the statesmen. But they could see nothing, because nothing was there.

'Now, if Your Imperial Majesty will be gracious enough to take off your clothes,' said the swindlers, 'then we will dress you in the new clothes right here in front of this big mirror.'

So the Emperor took off all his clothes, and the swindlers pretended to hand him each of the new garments they were supposed to have made. Then they made out they were zipping up the trousers and straightening the collar and draping the cloak.

'Wonderful! It's amazing how well they suit Your Majesty! What a terrific fit!' everyone started to say. 'What a pattern! What colours! What a gorgeous cloak!'

The Master of Ceremonies entered with an announcement. 'The canopy to be borne above Your Majesty in the procession has arrived outside.'

'Very well, I am ready,' said the Emperor. 'Don't they suit me down to the ground?' And he posed again in front of the mirror, trying to look as though he was gazing at his splendid new clothes.

The servants, who were to carry the cloak, stooped down and groped about on the floor, as if they were picking up the cloak; and as they walked they pretended to be holding something up in the air, not daring to let on that they couldn't see anything.

So the Emperor marched under the canopy in the Grand Procession, and all the people in the streets and hanging out of the windows said: 'Look! The Emperor's new clothes are the finest he has ever had! What a perfect fit! What a gorgeous cloak!' No one would let anyone else know that he couldn't see anything, because that would have meant he was unfit for his job or incredibly stupid. Never had the Emperor's clothes been such a howling success.

'But he's got nothing on!' shouted a little child.

'Good grief!' exclaimed the courtiers. 'Stupid child! His parents should take him home! It's ridiculous!' But the child's remark was whispered from one person to another.

'He's got nothing on! There's a little child saying he hasn't got anything on!'

'He hasn't got anything on!' shouted all the people at last. And the Emperor felt really uncomfortable, because it seemed to him that they were quite right. But somehow he thought to himself, 'Gosh, well, I must go through with it, procession and all.' So he drew himself proudly up to his full height, while his servants marched behind his behind, holding up the cloak that wasn't there.

Toby and the Wolf

A young miller hereabouts had a dog called Toby, passed down from his father. The old hound was getting long in the tooth, and had grown hard of hearing, so he couldn't guard the house as well as he used to. The miller neglected Toby, and the servants behaved as their master did. They gave Toby some shoe-leather whenever they passed him, and as often as not forgot to feed him. Toby had such a grim time of it, that he made up his mind to turn his back on the mill and chance his luck in the woods. On the way, he bumped into a wolf, who greeted him, '*Nazdar!* Comrade Toby! Where are you heading?'

The dog told him what he had to put up with back at the mill, and swore he would stick it no longer.

'Brother Toby,' said the wolf, 'you've got plenty of years, but precious little nous. Why leave the mill now, in your old age, and scrape a miserable existence in the woods? Twice, when you were young, you saved the mill from bandits, and now I'm hearing how disgracefully you've been treated! Take a tip from Wolfie, and go back to the mill and see to it that the miller feeds you properly.'

'Comrade Wolf,' said Toby, 'I would rather die of hunger than crawl back there.'

'Don't be so headstrong, Brother Toby,' said the wolf. 'Between us we'll find the answer to your problems! Now – tomorrow, when the nursemaid comes out to the field that the miller is harvesting, she'll be carrying his baby son. The moment she puts him down, I'll sneak up and make off with him. Your job is to sniff out my trail and follow it. I'll drop the brat in the grass beneath the great oak tree for you to find. Pick him up, take him back to the miller, and he'll greet you like a hero!'

The next day, the nursemaid went up to the field with food for the harvesters, and in one arm she was carrying the miller's baby son. When she reached the field, she laid the baby down on a sheaf and started up joking and flirting with the reapers. The wolf crept up, seized the infant, and sped away into the woods.

When the maid saw the wolf running for the trees with the baby in its jaws, she chased after it, sobbing and screaming for help, and too afraid to go home without her master's child. In the meantime, the harvesters had sent a lad sprinting back to the mill to tell the miller what had happened. Half out of his mind with distress, the miller rushed to fetch the hunter, and the pair of them legged it into the woods. But before they'd got very far, Toby appeared back at the mill, carrying the baby safely in his mouth. The miller's wife came running out, crying with joy, and she scooped up the baby and laid him in his cot. Then she patted and stroked Toby's head and ordered that bread and milk be set down before him at once.

When the miller came back and was told how Toby had saved his son, he felt so ashamed that he had neglected the old dog that he swore Toby would have nothing but the best from that day forward. And as the tale of the rescue spread, Toby was given a hero's welcome wherever he went.

One day, the wolf turned up to see Toby as he lay in the sun at the back of the mill. 'Admit it, Brother, how sound my advice was,' began the wolf. 'You live in the lap of plenty now, so don't forget! One good turn deserves another! I haven't eaten for a week and I need you to help me.'

Toby nodded. Then he said, 'No problem, Brother Wolf. One of the maids is to be married tomorrow and the pantry is stuffed full of meat and pastry and other good scoff for the wedding feast. Let's wait till dark: then we can get into the pantry through the back window and have a feast all of our own!'

So that evening, when darkness fell, the two cronies climbed through the pantry window. They stuffed and supped all night until the wolf grew reckless. 'Brother Toby!' he yelled. 'I'm so happy, I feel like a good old singsong!'

'You'd better shut up and get out of here quickly,' warned Toby, 'or we'll both be discovered and beaten!'

But the wolf had lost the plot and threw back his head with a wild wolf howl, and his racket could be heard all over the house. The miller woke up and searched every room in the mill before he remembered that the food for the wedding banquet was laid out in the pantry. He went to look and found Toby and the wolf. He snatched up a stick and laid into the two thieves, beating them until the hair flew from their pelts.

The wolf finally managed to escape, but the miller collared Toby and chained him up. In the morning, the miller's wife pleaded with him to let Toby off the chain, insisting that he must have been led astray by the wolf. So the miller removed the chain but warned Toby to keep well clear of the wolf.

Time passed, and late one night the wolf crept into the mill to persuade Toby to take revenge on the miller for the beating. Toby pointed out that the miller owned a powerful shotgun and could easily shoot them dead. But the wolf wouldn't be put off, and bragged of his strength and cunning.

'Ach, Brother Toby,' sneered the wolf, 'you're talking like a coward. I'm not going to leave this place with an empty belly. The miller owns a fat old ram. For old times' sake, I want you to drive it out of the flock for me. That way, I can kill it easily and eat my fill without any bother.'

Toby remembered the miller's warning about the wolf. Toby enjoyed his life at the mill now, and he had no desire to chuck it all away. But when he saw how angry the wolf was becoming, he grew scared of him and said, 'Brother Wolf, the ram would be certain to bleat and the miller will come running. You must stand in front of the sheep pen with your mouth open. When I drive the ram out, you must seize him by the head to stop him bleating and drag him off to the woods sharpish.'

The wolf was all for this and took up position outside the sheep pen. Toby jumped inside and drove the big strong ram towards the eager wolf. But the ram butted the wolf's butt and the wolf turned a somersault and crashed down in the yard, unable to move. He moaned and groaned, and wheezed, 'Brother Toby, the ram has knocked the breath out of my body! Keep him away from me!'

The miller heard the wolf crying. He saw the ram out in the yard and the wolf there too. He snatched up his shotgun and fired at the wolf. But although he hit him in the rear, the wolf managed to drag himself away.

Toby stretched out in his kennel, well pleased at the way matters had turned out. He told himself that he would never listen to the wolf again. But a few days later, what happened but the wolf turned up again at the mill to see Toby. 'We have to make the miller suffer for shooting at me,' he said. 'I have three pellets lodged in my arse. To get even with him, I'm going to destroy his favourite colt.'

Toby pleaded with the wolf not to do this, and said he would have no part in such a revenge. But the wolf bared his fangs at Toby. 'I will pin you down and sink my teeth into your scrawny throat if you refuse to help me,' he snarled. 'Do what I say this instant or you won't move from here alive. Drive the colt out of the stable so that I can fall upon it.'

The yard was deserted and Toby knew that he could never outwit the wolf or fight him off on his own. So he went into the stable and untied the colt. Then he called quietly to the wolf, 'Brother Wolf, make sure you bite the hind legs first!'

The wolf obeyed Toby, and the young horse kicked out at him with all its strength, which was exactly what Toby had planned. The wolf leaped to one side, howling and yowling in pain and rage, for the colt's hooves had knackered him badly. He made such a row that the miller heard him, and grabbing his shotgun, he rushed out into the yard and blasted the wolf dead.

Toby sighed with relief as he came out of the stable unharmed. The wolf could lead him into mischief no more and would never trouble him again. For the rest of his puff, Toby could look forward to living happy ever after in the sunshine.

The Juniper Tree

Once upon a time, that very old people can still remember, there lived a man and his good and beautiful wife. They loved each other so much that the only thing they wished for was a little child. Each night before sleep they prayed for a child, but none came and nothing changed.

There was a yard in front of their house and in the centre grew a juniper tree. One winter's day, the wife stood under the juniper tree peeling an apple, and as she was peeling it, she cut her finger and her blood wept onto the snow.

'Oh!' cried the wife, and she sighed deeply. She grew sad as she looked at the tears of blood on the snow. 'If only I had a child as red as blood and as white as snow.' These words seemed to lighten her mood and she felt a glow of cheerfulness as though something might happen. Then she went inside.

After a month, the snow was gone. After two months, everything was green. After three months, the earth grew flowers. After four months, the trees in the forest thickened and their green branches stretched and touched and intertwined. The birds began to sing and their songs tumbled from the trees among the falling blossom. Soon the fifth month had come and gone, and when the wife stood beneath the juniper tree, its sweet scent flooded her heart with happiness and she fell to her knees, pierced with joy. When the sixth month had passed, the fruit was full and swollen and she was serene. In the seventh month, she picked the juniper berries and ate them so obsessively that she became sick and moody. After the eighth month had passed, she pulled her husband to her and wept.

'If I die,' she cried, 'bury me under the juniper tree.'

After that, she was calm and contented until the ninth month was over. Then she had a child as red as blood and as white as snow. But when she looked at her baby for the first time, she was so ecstatic that she died.

Her husband buried her under the juniper tree and wept night and day. As time passed, he began to feel better, but there were still days when he cried. At last, he stopped, and after more suns and moons had gone, he found another wife. Together, he and his second wife had a daughter, while his child from his first wife was a little boy, who was as red as blood and as white as snow. Whenever the woman looked at her daughter, her heart bloomed with love for her. But when she looked at the boy, the same heart jerked with resentment. She knew that he would always be there to get in the way of her daughter inheriting everything. Then the devil gripped her and twisted her feelings towards the boy until she became very cruel to him. She jabbed him from here to there, slapped, slippered, clipped and cuffed him until the poor little boy was living in fear. When he came home after school, his life was hell.

One day, the woman went up to her room and her little girl came after her and asked, '*Mutter*, will you give me an apple?'

'*Ja, meine liebling*,' cooed the woman, and she chose her the most gorgeous apple from the chest, which had a heavy wooden lid and a big sharp iron lock.

'*Mutter*,' said the little daughter, 'shouldn't Brother have one too?'

The woman was annoyed at this, but she said, '*Ja*, when he gets back from school.' And when she looked out of the window and saw the boy coming, the devil tightened his hold on her, and she snatched the apple from her daughter.

'No apples until Brother is here,' she said and she threw the apple into the chest and shut the lid.

The little boy came in and the devil made her be friendly to him and say, 'Would you like a nice apple, *mein liebling*?' But she gave him a murderous look.

'*Mutter*,' said the boy, 'how fierce you look! Yes please, I would like an apple.'

Then something made her entice him.

'Come here, come here,' she coaxed, as she lifted the lid. 'Choose an apple for yourself.'

And as the boy bent over the chest, the devil possessed her, and – *bang!* – she slammed down the lid so hard that his little head flew off and rolled among the apples. The woman went cold with fear and thought, 'How will I get away with this?' She flew up to her room, rushed to her dresser and yanked out a white neckerchief. She balanced the boy's head back on his neck and tied the neckerchief around his throat so that nothing could be seen. Then she propped him in a chair in front of the door and twisted an apple into his hand.

A little while later, little Marlene came into the scullery and tugged at her mother, who was stirring, stirring, stirring a pot of boiling water in front of the fire.

'*Mutter*,' said Marlene, 'Brother is sitting by the door and he has turned very pale. He's got an apple in his hand, but when I asked him to give me the apple he wouldn't reply, and now I'm frightened!'

'Go back to him,' said the woman, 'and if he still won't answer you, give him a good clout on the ear.'

Little Marlene went back to him and said, 'Brother, give me the apple.'

But he said nothing. Nothing. So she fetched him a box on the ear and his head fell off. The little girl was so terrrified that she began to weep and wail. Then she ran to her Mother and said, 'Oh, *Mutter*, I've knocked my brother's head off.' And she cried and cried and could not be comforted.

'Oh, Marlene,' said the woman, 'what have you done!

You'd better keep quiet about this. No one must ever know. And anyway, there's precious little we can do about it now. We'd best make a stew out of him.'

So the mother got the little boy and chopped him into pieces. Then she tossed them into a pot and let them simmer and steam and stew. Marlene stood close by, sobbing, and her tears splashed onto the stew so it did not need any salt.

When the father came home from work, he sat down at the table and asked, 'Where is my son?'

The woman dished up a huge, steamy serving of the stew, and Marlene wept and wept and wept,

'Where's my son?' the father demanded again.

'Oh,' said the woman, 'he's away to the countryside to visit his mother's great uncle. They'll look after him well.'

'Oh, this has upset me,' said the father. 'It's all wrong. He should have said goodbye to me.' Then he began to eat the stew, but said, 'Marlene, what are you blubbing about? Your brother will be home soon enough.' Still munching heartily, he said, 'Wife, this food is delicious! Dish me up some more!' And the more he ate, the more he wanted. 'More!' he said. 'Give me some more! I'm not sharing a scrap of it. Somehow I feel this has got my name on it!'

As he chomped and chewed, he chucked the bones under the table until he was stuffed. But Marlene slipped to her dresser and fetched her best silk neckerchief from the bottom drawer. She tenderly gathered up all the bones from beneath the table, tied up in her silk kerchief and carried them outside. Her tears were bitter as she placed the bones beneath the juniper tree. But as she laid them there, she felt suddenly consoled, and the tears dried on her cheeks. And now the juniper tree rustled and moved. The branches parted and joined, parted and joined, as though they were clapping their hands with joy. At the same time, smoke drifted out of the tree, and in the heart of the smoke there was a brightly burning fire. Then a wonderful bird flapped from the flames and began singing beautifully. He soared higher and higher into the air, and when he had disappeared, the juniper tree was just as it was before. But the silk neckerchief was gone. Marlene felt very light and happy. It was as though her brother was still alive, and she went gaily back into the house, sat down at the table, and ate.

Meanwhile, the bird flew away, landed on a goldsmith's house, and began to sing:

Meine mutter, she killed me.
Mein vater, he ate me.
My sister, Marlene,
Made certain to gather
My bones all together,
In silk wrapped so nicely,
Under the juniper tree.
Tweet-tweet!
Under the juniper tree.
Tweet-tweet!
What a beautiful bird I am!

The goldsmith was busy in his workshop, crafting a golden chain. He heard the bird singing on his roof and thought the sound was beautiful. He stood up to go outside, and as he crossed the threshold he lost a slipper. But he kept on walking, right into the middle of the road, with only one sock and a slipper on. He was also wearing his work apron, and in one hand he held the golden chain and in the other his tongs. The sun sparkled on the street as he walked and then he stopped to get a good look at the bird.

'Bird,' he said, 'you sing so beautifully! Please sing me that song again.'

'No,' said the bird, 'I don't sing twice for nothing. Give me the golden chain and I'll sing it for you once more.'

'It's a deal,' said the goldsmith. 'Here's the golden chain. Now sing that lovely song again.'

The bird swooped down, scooped up the golden chain in his right claw, stood before the goldsmith and began singing:

Meine mutter she killed me.
Mein vater he ate me.
My sister, Marlene,
Made certain to gather
My bones all together,
In silk wrapped so nicely
Under the juniper tree.
Tweet-tweet!
Under the juniper tree.
Tweet-tweet!
What a beautiful bird I am.

Then the bird flapped away to a shoemaker's house, perched on his roof and sang:

Meine mutter she killed me.
Mein vater he ate me.
My sister, Marlene,
Made certain to gather
My bones all together,
In silk wrapped so nicely
Under the juniper tree.
Tweet-tweet!
Under the juniper tree.
Tweet-tweet!
What a beautiful bird I am.

When the shoemaker heard the song, he ran to the door in his singlet and squinted up at the roof, shielding his eyes from the bright sun with his hand.

'Bird,' he said, 'you sing so beautifully!' Then he called into the house. 'Wife! Come outside for a moment. There's a bird up there. Look! He sings so beautifully!' Then he called his daughter and her children, and the apprentices and the maid. They all came hot-footing out into the street to squinny up at the bird, and they saw how truly beautiful he was. He had vivid bright feathers of red and green; his neck glistened like gold, and his eyes sparkled and shone in his head like stars.

'Bird,' said the shoemaker. 'Please sing me that song again.'

'No,' said the bird. 'I don't sing twice for nothing. You'll have to give me a present.'

'Wife,' said the man, 'go into the shop. You'll see a pair of red shoes on the top shelf. Fetch them here.'

His wife hurried and returned with the shoes.

'There you go!' said the man. 'Now sing that lovely song again.'

The bird swooped down, scooped up the shoes in his left claw, flew back onto the roof, and sang:

Meine mutter she killed me.
Mein vater he ate me.
My sister, Marlene,
Made certain to gather
My bones all together,
In silk wrapped so nicely
Under the juniper tree.
Tweet-tweet!
Under the juniper tree.
Tweet-tweet!
What a beautiful bird I am!

When the song was finished, the bird fluttered away. He clutched the gold chain in his right claw and the red shoes in his left, and he flew far away to a mill. *Clickety-clack-*

clack-clack, clickety-clack-clack-clack went the mill. The miller had twenty fellows working in the mill, and they were all hewing a millstone. *Chick-chack, chick-chack, chick-chack* went twenty chisels. And the mill kept saying *clickety-clack-clack-clack, clickety-clack-clack-clack*. The bird flew down and perched on a linden tree outside the mill and sang:

Meine mutter she killed me.

the men stopped working.

Mein vater he ate me.

Then two more downed tools and listened.

My sister, Marlene,
Made certain to gather . . .

Then four more stopped.

. . . My bones all together,
In silk wrapped so nicely . . .

Now only eight chaps were chiselling.

. . . Under the juniper tree.
Tweet-tweet!

Now only five.

. . . under the juniper tree.
Tweet-tweet!

Now only one.

What a beautiful bird I am!

Then the last chiseller chucked chiselling and listened to the final words.

'Bird,' he said, 'you sing so beautifully! Let me hear it all! Sing your song to me again.'

'No,' answered the bird. 'I don't sing twice for nothing. Give me the millstone and then I'll sing it for you again.'

'I would give it to you if I could,' said the man. 'But the millstone doesn't just belong to me.'

'If he sings the song again,' chorused his workmates, 'we'll give him the stone.'

So the bird swooped down and the twenty miller's men grabbed beams to lift the stone. 'Heave-ho! Heave-ho!' The bird pushed his neck through the hole and wore the stone like a collar. Then he flew back to the tree and sang:

Meine mutter she killed me.
Mein vater he ate me.
My sister Marlene
Made certain to gather
My bones all together,
In silk wrapped so nicely,
Under the juniper tree.
Tweet-tweet!
Under the juniper tree.
Tweet-tweet!
What a beautiful bird I am!

The bird finished the song and spread his wings. In his right claw, he had the chain, in his left the shoes, and around his neck the millstone. Then he flew away to the Father's house.

The father, the mother and Marlene were sitting at the table in the parlour, and the father cried, 'Hurrah! I'm so happy! I feel absolutely wonderful!'

'I don't, I don't,' said the mother. 'I feel scared, as though a huge storm was brewing.'

Marlene sat there and wept and wept and wept. Then the bird flew over and, as he landed on the roof, the father said, 'Oh, I'm in such a good mood! The sun is shining at its brightest and I feel just as though I were going to meet an old friend again!'

'I don't, I don't,' said his wife. 'I'm so frightened that my teeth are rattling in my head. My blood's in flames in my veins.'

She ripped her bodice from her breast, and Marlene huddled in the corner and wept and wept. She held her handkerchief to her eyes and cried until it was sodden with her tears. The bird swooped down to the juniper tree, where he perched on a branch and began singing:

Meine mutter she killed me.

The Mother covered her ears, squeezed shut her eyes, and tried to see and hear nothing, but there was a roaring in her head like a huge thunderstorm, and her eyes spat and flashed like lightning.

Mein vater he ate me.

'Oh, *Mutter*,' said the Father, 'listen to how beautifully that bird sings. The sun's so warm and it smells of cinammon.'

My sister, Marlene,
Made certain . . .

Marlene put her head on her knees and wept and wept, but the man said, 'I'm going outside. I have to see this bird close-up.'

'Don't go!' gasped the wife. 'I feel as though the whole house is shaking and ready to burst into flames!'

But the man went outside and looked at the bird.

. . . to gather
My bones all together,
In silk wrapped so nicely,
Under the juniper tree.
Tweet-tweet!
Under the juniper tree.
Tweet-tweet!
What a beautiful bird I am!

The bird finished his song and dropped the golden chain so that it fell neatly around the man's neck and fitted him perfectly. The man went inside and said, 'Look how wonderful that bird is! He gave me this gorgeous golden chain and he's just as gorgeous himself!'

But the woman was petrified and collapsed to the floor. Her cap fell from her head and the bird sang again:

Meine mutter, she killed me.

'Aah! I wish I was a thousand feet under the earth and not have to hear this song!'

Mein vater, he ate me.

Then the woman fell to the floor again as if she was dead.

My sister, Marlene, made certain . . .

'Oh!' said Marlene. 'I want to go outside as well and see if the bird will give me something too!' So she went out.

. . . to gather
My bones all together,
In silk wrapped so nicely . . .

Then the bird threw her the shoes.

. . . under the juniper tree.
Tweet-tweet!
Under the juniper tree.
Tweet-tweet!
What a beautiful bird I am!

Marlene felt light and happy. She slipped her feet into the new red shoes and skipped back into the house.

'Hurrah!' she said 'The bird is so wonderful! He gave me these red shoes as a present! When I went outside I felt so sad, but now I feel full of joy!'

'I don't, I don't,' gasped the wife. She leapt to her feet and her hair flared and crackled like the red flames of hell. 'I feel as if the end of the world is coming! I must get outside!'

So she rushed out of the door and *crash!* the bird threw the millstone down on her head and she was crushed to death. The father and Marlene heard the terrible noise and ran outside. Black smoke and red flames were dancing on the spot, and when it was finished the little brother stood there alive. He took hold of his father's hand and Marlene's hand and the three of them were overjoyed. They went into the house, sat down at the table, and started to eat.

The Girl and the North Wind

High up in the mountains of Norway a girl lived with her mother. The girl's name was Kari and one day her mother asked her to fetch the flour to bake loaves and biscuits. Kari seized the biggest bowl in the kitchen and ran willingly to the barn. She filled the bowl right to the top and hurried back across the yard when – *whish-whoosh!* – the North Wind swaggered around the corner and scattered all the flour away with one great puff.

Kari went back to the barn, refilled the bowl, and hastened across the yard when – *whish-whoosh!* – up rushed the North Wind again and blew away all the flour. Yet again Kari went to the barn. She scooped up all the flour that was left, which wasn't even enough to reach halfway up the bowl, and hugged it to her as she bolted across the yard. But – *whish-whoosh!* – around the corner bowled the North Wind and puffed away the flour.

'It'll be gruel for the whole winter now,' scolded Kari's mother. 'There'll be no bread and definitely no biscuits till next year.'

'No bread? No *biscuits*?' gasped Kari. 'Well, I'm going to get the flour back!' And before her mother could draw breath she ran out of the door.

All that day Kari crunched and trudged through the snow until at last she reached the place where the North Wind lived.

'North Wind! Come out here! I want to talk to you! Now!' shouted Kari and she thumped on the door as loudly as she could.

After a few minutes the North Wind opened the door, scratching himself and yawning. 'What's all this banging and bawling? How can I have a decent kip with all this commotion?'

'You stole our flour!' exclaimed Kari. 'You breezed up to our house – *ehn, too, treh* – three times today and blew away all our flour and now we won't have any bread all winter and we'll probably starve to death and it'll be All Your Fault!'

The North Wind's face puckered and wrinkled. 'I do apologise,' he said in a big blustery voice. 'Sometimes I get completely carried away with blowing. I meant no harm, but it's impossible for me to get your flour back now.' He stared at the girl for a moment. Then he added, 'I can't give you your flour back, but I can give you something else.'

He disappeared inside and returned holding a cloth. 'This cloth is magic. All you have to do is say, "Cloth, cloth, spread yourself and set out scrumptious scram," and you will have all the food and drink you can imagine.'

Kari thanked the North Wind, pocketed the cloth, and set off homewards. It was getting dark, but Kari came to an inn on the road and decided to stay the night there. She knocked on the door and it swung open at once. Out hobbled a troll crone whose warty nose was so long she had tucked it into her waistband to avoid tripping.

'*Goo kuelh*,' rasped the crone in a haggy voice.

'*Goo kuelh*, good evening,' faltered Kari. 'I was wondering, please may I have a bed for the night?'

'How will you pay for it?' growled the troll crone.

'I am afraid I have no money. But I can feed you and your guests.'

'How?'

Kari took out the cloth, gave it a shake, holding it at both ends, and said, 'Cloth, cloth, spread yourself and set out scrumptious scram!'

At once the cloth was groaning with food – soups and soufflés, roasts and stews, steaks and sausages, pies and flans, fruits and vegetables, trifles and puddings, and every kind of drink.

When all the guests at the inn had filled their boots, Kari rolled up her cloth and went to bed. But at dead of night, when everyone was in the land of nod, the troll crone came creeping up the stairs with a cloth identical to Kari's. She sneaked into her room and swapped her cloth for hers.

Next morning, Kari woke up, snatched the cloth and sprinted all the way home. 'Mama! Mama! Look what the North Wind gave me,' she shouted excitedly. She babbled out the magic words and shook the cloth. Nothing! She tried again – and again – and again – twisting the cloth this way and that, but nothing worked.

'The North Wind has tricked me!' said Kari furiously and she marched off to the North Wind's house before her mother could say no.

'North Wind! Come outside! I want to talk to you!' bawled Kari at the door. After a while, the North Wind emerged, rubbing his eyes sleepily.

'You again?' he yawned. 'Why are you back so soon?'

'You know very well why I'm back!' yelled Kari, almost in tears. 'The cloth you gave me was useless! It only worked once and what good is that?'

'Just the once? Something is wrong,' said the North Wind. 'But let's not quarrel. I'll give you something else.' Soon enough he came back with an old goat.

'This goat is magic. All you have to do is say, "Goat! Splosh! Crip, crap, dosh!" and it will make all the money you need.'

'Will it work more than once?' asked Kari suspiciously.

'For ever,' promised the North Wind.

So Kari took the goat and set off homewards. It was getting dark so she decided to return to the inn for the night. She knocked on the door and the troll crone swung it open at once. Broth dripped from her huge conk because she'd been using it to stir her soup-pot.

'*Goo kuelh*, good evening. I was wondering if I could have a bed for tonight?' said Kari.

'How are you going to pay?' rattled the crone.

Kari turned to the old goat and said, 'Goat! Splosh! Crip, crap, dosh!' Immediately, out of its backside, dropped a jackpot of gold coins. Kari paid the crone, used another sovereign for food and drink, and then went to bed. In the middle of the night, the troll crone once more came crawling up the stairs, this time with her own goat, which she switched for Kari's.

When Kari got home next day, she tried to show her mother just what the goat could do. But whatever came out of *this* old goat's rear end certainly wasn't gold!

Kari stomped back to the North Wind, more livid than ever. The North Wind just scratched at his flowing silvery mane, tossed it, and said, 'Something is wrong. I'll give you one last thing, but you'd better use it wisely.' Off he went and back he came with a stick. 'This stick is magic. All you have to do is say "Stick, stick, lay on!" and it will thrash anyone you want. When you want it to stop, just say "Stick, stick, lay off!" and it will come straight back to you.'

Kari thanked the North Wind and went straight to the Inn.

'*Goo kuelh*,' cawed the troll crone.

'May I have a bed for the night?'

'How do you plan to pay?' growled the crone, leering at the stick. Kari found some spare coins in her apron and went straight to bed.

In the dark small hours, the crone came creeping up the stairs again. She was certain the stick was magic. Slowly she sneaked into the room. Just as she was about to swap her stick for Kari's, up Kari jumped and bellowed, 'Stick, stick, lay on!'

The stick whizzed from the pillow and began to give the troll crone such a hiding that she danced from one foot to the other all over the room, howling and hooting and hollering, until at last she screeched, 'Make it stop! Make it stop!'

'Not until you give me back my cloth and my goat,' shouted Kari.

'I will, I will!' shrieked the troll crone.

'Stick, stick, lay off,' ordered Kari and at once the stick flew – *whish-whoosh* – into her hand. But she kept a firm grip on it as she marched behind the troll crone to fetch her cloth and her goat.

The next morning, Kari ran home with her treasures, and with them she and her mother had all the food and money and protection they needed for the rest of their long and extremely happy lives.

Snipp, snapp, snute,
Her er eventyret ute!
Snip, snap, snut,
My gob's now shut!